The Zne

how to get in it
and stay in it

TOM EVANS

THE ZONE : HOW TO GET IN IT AND STAY IN IT

1st edition, published 2013
ISBN 978-1-849-14370-7

Front cover background ©LuckyDesigner, Hexagon Puzzle ©Jjava and Magnifying Glass ©James Chipper. The image of The Hermit used with kind permission of the Builders of the Adytum.

Book Layout ©2013 BookDesignTemplates.com

Published by Tmesis Ltd | www.tmesis.co

Contents

GUIDANCE TO ALL EXPLORERS.
CARRY A STAFF TO KEEP YOU STEADY
AND A LIGHT TO SHOW
YOU AND OTHERS THE WAY ...

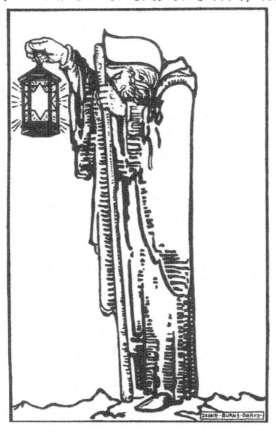

FORE WORDS

This book is a revelation and it is revolutionary.

If you are not one to normally read personal development books, this will change your mind and make your world spin on its axis.

The language is simple and concise. The explanations are clear.

Be prepared for an illuminating journey from the No Zone to the Go Zone.

About The Zone

THE ZONE IS A MAGICAL SPACE WHERE WE ARE SUPER-CREATIVE AND SUPER-PRODUCTIVE.

Our performances are effortless when we are in it. Our creative output is perfection itself when we are in The Zone. We love watching our sports women and men, or our favourite singer or band, when they are at the top of their game and 'on fire'. We feel for them if they are off form.

Just imagine, in business, what it would be like if clients just find you, just when you need them. When you are in The Zone, times of hardship and struggle fast become a distant memory. In our personal lives, when you are in The Zone, you tend to be surrounded by supportive friends and families. You also tend to form longer lasting, more stable relationships.

If you find yourself out of The Zone, it can be a lonely place to be. You might wonder what you have done wrong to deserve your lot in life.

When you are in The Zone however, by far the best aspect of being there is that it's nicely infectious. When you are in it, you cannot help but pull in those around you.

The first part of this book explores how we perform when we make things happen when we inhabit the Doing Zones. These are zones where we are at our creative and productive peaks.

By way of contrast, the second part of the book takes us on a journey into the Danger Zones. These are places we end up in, from time to time, where nothing goes right for us, despite our best efforts. We must beware when we find ourselves in these dark corners and cul-de-sacs, as our friends and colleagues can all too easily end up in there with us.

The concluding section is a doorway into another world and a new way of being. Just imagine what your life might be like if you were permanently in the Being Zones. Imagine a world where everything happens magically and good fortune knocks at your door every day.

At the end of each chapter in the Doing and Being Zones, you'll find suggestions on Zoning In still further. At the end of each Danger Zone chapter, there's tips on Zoning Out, as a route back to getting on an even keel.

This book has been constructed in a special and magical fashion. As such, it can be read in several ways.

For example, it works equally well if you read it backwards as well as forwards. You can read about a category of zones at a time, again either backwards or forwards.

You can simply dip in and out of the book, sampling an individual zone at a time.

Zones, as you will see, are what we make them. While they have walls and boundaries, they can also have doors and windows so they can be open or closed. We can also form enlarged Super Zones from any number of zones.

Such is the magic that unfolds when you enter The Zone.

[2]

In the Zone

WE ALL LIKE TO BE 'IN THE ZONE'. EVERYTHING HAPPENS SO MAGICALLY WHEN WE ARE THERE.

We love it too when our sports women and men perform at their peak, when they are in that 'special place'. They make it look so easy when they reach these lofty heights in their sport, such is their discipline, training and natural propensity for their craft.

When a golfer is on their game, they just know where the ball is going as soon as they take the back swing - or indeed before they step up to take their shot. Footballers kind of know if they are going to score or miss a penalty when they spot the ball. The finalists in the 100 metres all know who is coming first and last before the gun goes off. Fates are sealed in the minds of the performers well before the performance itself takes place.

Artists, musicians and writers just know when they are on to a good thing. When crafting their art, they enter a timeless place with a seamless connection to their Muse.

It is like another intelligence has taken control and they are just the medium and channel for the imagery, soundscape or words that are coming their way. Everything becomes effortless.

Sometimes too it takes others to notice we're on fire as we are so 'in the zone' and everything else is defocussed. It just feels natural to us until we find ourselves unwittingly 'out of the zone'.

SO WE KNOW WHEN WE ARE IN THE ZONE AND WE KNOW WHEN WE ARE OUT OF IT BUT WHERE EXACTLY IS IT?

HOW DO WE FIND OUR WAY THERE?

HOW DO WE KNOW WHEN WE ARE IN IT?

HOW CAN SOME PEOPLE JUST GET IN IT SO EASILY?

WHEN WE ARE OUT OF IT, HOW DO WE GET BACK IN THERE?

Sometimes, a good place to start any such journey is a dictionary. The dictionary definitions tell us that a zone is a noun that describes places and regions with clearly defined edges and boundaries. A zone is defined as having a geographical or spatial nature. Note, in passing, that we can also use the word as a verb to 'zone something off'.

We can park in certain zones and sometimes get fined if we don't.

Our brains get a little confused if we swap time zones too quickly.

Frustratingly though, these definitions give us no clue at all as to 'the zone' we get into when everything is flowing with ease and we are performing at our peak. They tell us little about how to 'zone in' or when to 'zone out'.

This is because the zones that we are in when we are on form are less tangible than this. For these somewhat mythical zones, there is no Border Control and we can slip in and out of them without a passport. Neither is there a map telling us where this zone actually is and how to hope to even get there. It is this lack of any map that leads to us often not even being aware we were in the zone until after we were in it, or when we know we are out of it.

This book is an attempt at crafting this map. Like all maps it is only a model and a work in progress. Explorers who use it will find other places worth visiting and may even spot some errors. As the territory changes over time, the map will almost certainly need updating. In fact, we will also need more than one map as there is not just one zone but many.

We find that many of the zones also comprise of sub-zones. These are attributes, qualities and shades that we can adopt when in a particular zone.

At the same time, many of the zones are complementary and can be joined together to build bigger, more powerful zones.

We can even take one of the Danger Zones and neutralise its effect by surrounding it with Doing and Being Zones.

This is of course analogous to what happens with real zones and territories. If we share our border with those who are belligerent, we may get absorbed into a hostile zone, which is potentially unhealthy for us. If we live in a small town where all the neighbours are friendly, the kindness and happiness spreads. When we work with people who are creative and entrepreneurial, we cannot help but to pick up on their energy.

Zones are dynamic places with constantly changing edges. Like the cells in our body, they can replicate and grow healthily or mutate into less desirable forms. Like all living things, the zones we inhabit benefit from care and attention.

[3]

Out of the Zone

WHEN WE STRAY OUT OF THE ZONE, WE MAY FIND
WE HAVE WANDERED INTO THE DANGER ZONES.

These zones can suck us in when we are least aware. Once in, we can be stuck there for days, months or even years. Some people spend a whole life time in one or more of the Danger Zones. These unfortunate souls are easy to spot. They are the naysayers who constantly worry or pour scorn on anything that is in the least bit positive. Misfortune seems to visit their door more often than Lady Luck. They are quite often ill.

Sometimes entry into the Danger Zones are triggered by an external event. Someone may have annoyed you at work or crossed a boundary. An accident or illness may have afflicted a family member. You may have been doing brilliantly in one of the Doing Zones when all the wheels came off. This can of course lead to all sorts of emotions like self-doubt, guilt and anger.

In each case though, it is our reaction to the event, not the event itself that causes us to be entrapped in a Danger Zone.

While we might not be able to define or locate 'the zone', we can easily spot when we are out of it.

For starters, our language gives it away.

> *"I am out of sorts."*
>
> *"The world is against me today."*
>
> *"I can't get out of the blocks this morning."*
>
> *"I wish there were more hours in the day."*

This latter statement especially is such a tell tale sign that things are not going our way.

So when we are 'out of the zone', it appears that the world, the system, our colleagues at work, our friends and even our family are against us. We can become indignant and even angry. It is all too easy to end up in a downward spiral of depression and alienation. This makes it increasingly difficult to get back 'in the zone'.

Just imagine for a moment a time when everything was going swimmingly. You were on fire and unstoppable. What ever you were doing at the time, you were focussed on the task at hand and your mind was not occupied in self absorption. Perhaps after the event you were glowing with pride at what you had done and achieved with such ease.

If you think of a past conversation though, or daydream about making millions on the back of what you are working on, such mind wanderings will take you 'out of the zone'.

The best aspect of being in The Zone is that, when you are in it, you cannot help but suck those around you into it too. We must beware as, when we are in a Danger Zone, we adversely affect our friends, family and colleagues. Critics and journalists can exhibit this tendency. They hover like hungry vultures, when celebrities encounter misfortune, looking for scraps to feed on and distribute to equally voracious readers.

We possess an inner critic which can be all too active at times. Our mind gets clouded in self pity causing in turn a lack of self worth. When this happens we are simply unable to perform at our best.

The solution though is not as simple as snapping out of it. We know that time can heal rifts but we often want a solution right away. How do we go about it?

What we need is some perspective. This is not as simple as seeing the world as being 'a glass half full', as opposed to being 'a glass half empty'. Of course, we know there are many people worse off than us and that we should be grateful for what we've got. If someone tells you that, it can make the situation worse, not better. What we need is help to get back in the zone now.

For starters, it helps to look at adversity and resistance from a different viewpoint. Look for what it teaches you about you and what you can learn from it.

For example, if you work out how to get over the barrier that is stopping you, then you can turn such adversity into opportunity. You can write a book about what you learned, start running workshops and deliver personal mentoring to those similarly afflicted. You have been there and got the T-shirt so you are well placed to help others.

More simply, we can take such an adversity and see it as a sign we are going about things the wrong way. When you get to the end of this book and enter the Magic Zone, it is my aim for readers to discover a much easier way to be, to do, to think and to feel.

So right now, if you are feeling 'out of the zone' the best thing you can do is to say "Thank You!". Thank whoever might be your god, or just the Universe, for bringing this realisation to your attention.

Doing Z🔍nes

DOING ZONES ARE WHERE WE SHOW THE
WORLD WHAT WE ARE MADE OF.

THEY ARE WHERE WE PERFORM.

THEY ARE WHERE WE PRODUCE.

THEY ARE WHERE WE MAKE WAVES.

THEY ARE WHERE WE FIND OUR NICHE.

THEY ARE WHERE WE SHINE OUR LIGHT.

[4]

The Performance Zone

THE GREAT THING ABOUT PERFORMING LIVE IS THAT WHEN IT'S OVER, IT'S OVER. THERE'S NO NEED TO DO IT AGAIN.

The worst thing about performing live is that when it's over, it's over and there's no chance to do it again. We only get one shot at it.

So, faced with this predicament, one of the best ways we can ensure we never mess up, it not to put ourselves 'out there'. This is evident when you look at the ratio of performers to watchers on the planet.

In a sports arena, you may have 20 to 40 performing, a few hundred support staff and tens of thousands of spectators. In a concert hall, you might see a group of 5 to 15 musicians or actors, with an audience in their hundreds or low thousands. There may of course be millions or even billions of faceless watchers on TV.

Even at a school play, a couple of handfuls of brave and aspiring children may be watched by 10 to 100 of their shy and retiring peers, along with doting parents recording the event for posterity and their child's potential embarrassment later in life.

You can see that the bug for entering the performance zone is often caught early. What is also all too easily picked up early on is an aversion to be in the spotlight.

The key to being able to perform without effort lies with being confident about our our ability to shine. Somewhat ironically this means we stop acting and pretending so that the 'real us' is seen out there. This congruency is something that the audience picks up on both consciously and unconsciously.

We just know when someone is performing at the top of their game. We know too when they are faking it or not giving 100%. By the way, despite the insistence of talent show judges, both mathematically and semantically if someone was able to give 110%, a thousand or even a million percent, all they have done is recalibrate what their personal 100% represents.

So how do we get to this special place where we are both comfortable and confident to get out there and strut our stuff?

Well here's where the six sub-zones for the Performance Zone come in. Each live performance represents the tip of an iceberg and the graciousness of the swan above the water. Hours and hours of practice and preparation goes towards every minute in the spotlight. Behind the scene, lots of paddling has taken place.

DESIRE

All performers must have an inner desire for the activity they aspire to excel in. This is what gets them up in the morning.

If their chosen activity is one they enjoy, and hopefully one that they can make money from, then this is a real bonus.

You will have heard the phrase, "When you love what you do, you will never work again." Being paid for what you love doing, and are passionate about, is a fabulous carrot to get you into and to keep you in the Performance Zone.

COMPETITION

Some people love the thrill of competition and the idea of coming first. Whether this is healthy or not is not of prime concern here. One inherent aspect of our nature is survival of the fittest and when we compete, drugs are released in our body to give us a natural high and to help us perform at our peak. These drugs are of course addictive and, as a result, some people get hooked with competition. Incidentally, the same drugs get released in the audience who might not be expending the same amount of energy to work them through their system.

Two byproducts of such empathy are crowd violence and obesity. So while competition is to be encouraged to help us in the Performance Zone, we should be mindful of its consequences.

PERSISTENCE

When you get addicted to being in the Performance Zone, it is almost par for the course that you end up flat on your face at some time.

Even Usain Bolt has had his false starts.

One essential quality of any performer is the ability to pick up the pieces and start again. While this can be immensely difficult at the time, it is obvious that such persistence is what separates the top performers from the also rans.

Every time you come back from a poor performance, you can potentially return both stronger and wiser. Indeed, if you are competing against others, they may have yet to make the same mistakes that you have.

This can be used as a strength and many sports people play mind and body games as part of their strategy. A tennis player might throw a game, or even a set, by appearing to be tired only to come back with all guns blazing and then stunning their opponent.

INCENTIVE

If we are going to put ourselves in an exposed and potentially threatening position, it's nice to have that carrot on a stick to drag us out there. The obvious incentive is money and, for some, both fame and recognition. This has both positive and negative ramifications. If we are very desperate for money, should we fail, the worry about the lack of it might cause desperation.

Acting recklessly then might subsequently lead to failure. If we get too much of it, it can go to our head and lead to a hedonistic life style, which could become unhealthy. The key of course is balance.

There is however an opportunity to seek a higher incentive which could lead to bigger and more sustainable rewards.

The performer who keeps going from childhood all the way to old age is rare. The odd crooner, actor or even golfer may manage to pull it off but, where physical fitness is a must, running shoes and football boots get hung up relatively early. So performing with altruism for your craft gives a level of incentive which is somewhat ageless.

This leads to opportunities to mentor new, up and coming talent. Actors therefore become directors and sports people become coaches and team managers. Those that make this transition will indeed have money on their mind but also carry a passion that incentivises them.

Training

The main reason why top performers make everything look so effortless is because they have practiced their routines many times. They will have had hours of training, some of which may have been formal and some just experiential.

Neuroscientists are starting to understand how our brains operate when tackling repetitive tasks. Firstly we have special structures in our brain that copy the behaviour of others. They are imaginatively called "mirror neurons". So simply by watching others, or yourself, perform a task over and over again, we can prime ourselves to repeat it with more ease.

The true function of the left and right hemispheres is also becoming clearer. It's not so much that the left brain is logical and the right creative.

Rather, areas in the left brain store learned and repetitive tasks and focus on detail, whereas the right brain tends to process new tasks and looks at the whole.

So for any performer to operate effortlessly, the process they follow must be engrained in their neurology from hours of repetitive practice. Their right brain should be on the alert for aspects of overall strategy while the left brain pays attention to any items of detail.

By using the whole brain on a task something remarkable happens. We stop having to pay attention to the what and how of any task. We then move to a position of unconscious competence, where we are solely focussed on outcome.

VISUALISATION

By seeing a successful outcome, whether it be winning a race or wowing an audience with our performance, we elevate ourselves to a position of higher perspective.

This is why visualisation of such outcomes is a tool used by sports psychologists and performance coaches.

We can also visualise the minutiae of a performance such as how we pull back a snooker cue, or how to stick our neck a centimetre further forward as we cross the line in a sprint finish.

This type of visualisation strengthens the neural pathways in our brain and our bodies. In turn, this helps to reinforce the learned responses so we can simply focus on delivery of that perfect performance.

ZONING IN

Now while we have been largely looking at sports and stage performances here, each one of us has to perform in some capacity every day. Whether we are performing at work or in our social life, exactly the same principles apply.

All activities are best approached with a desire to complete them. So say you are undertaking a mundane task you really don't like, you could use your imagination to introduce some fun into it. An example might be to introduce an element of healthy competition, even if it is with yourself. Perhaps doing it faster or with more 'joie de vivre' might help.

Being persistent when others give up will pay dividends in good time. Giving yourself an incentive here will undoubtedly help.

With training comes new learning and the ability to delegate tasks to our unconscious mind. Our conscious mind simply visualises the desired outcome.

When you put all of this together, you can almost sit back, relax and enjoy delivering your own performances with grace and ease.

[5]

The Entrepreneurial Zone

IT TAKES A SPECIAL PERSON TO ENTER THE ENTREPRENEURIAL ZONE. ONLY EXTRA SPECIAL PEOPLE THOUGH CAN STAY IN IT FOR ANY LENGTH OF TIME.

Some people are born entrepreneurs of course. They can be spotted early on in their lives. In the playground at school, they can be found making trades furtively in the corner. In times gone by they might be exchanging football cards. Nowadays their nose might be stuck in a smartphone and they could be plying their trade on eBay anywhere on the planet.

Other people find themselves inadvertently in the Entrepreneurial Zone later in life. Perhaps an early redundancy takes the rug from under their feet and catapults them into launching a new business.

Once you get in this zone, it's addictive. You begin to live on the edge, perhaps not knowing how or when your bills might get paid.

You push boundaries by going places and doing things never done before. You find the zone full of interesting and eclectic characters. Some are visionaries; some are revolutionaries; some are just bonkers.

It's the etymology of the word that gives some insight into the essential nature of an entrepreneur.

In recent history, it comes from the old French verb 'entreprendre' meaning 'to undertake'. It maybe apocryphal but it's thought that it has even earlier roots in the phrase from Sanskrit 'Antha Prerna' meaning 'self motivated'.

It's unquestionable, entrepreneurs have to be 'self-motivated' and they have to 'undertake' all manner of things. Entrepreneurs are human too and suffer bouts of self doubt and sometimes from hard times. Each entrepreneur has an angel on one shoulder driving them forward. On the other sits a devil telling not to be so silly and to go and get a day job.

What separates those who survive in this zone from those who struggle is mindset. This is not as trivial as holding that optimistic 'glass half full' mentality in the face of adversity. In fact, the most successful entrepreneurs positively thrive in the face of adversity.

When they struggle over something, or see others having a hard time, they know if they come up with a solution to solve this problem, they will be on to a winner. Especially if that winner saves or makes those who invest in it more than it costs them.

They are the people who undertake to do something that others before have not dared to do or even thought to do.

An entrepreneur by nature must be multi-faceted. They are required to be both a polymath and jack of all trades while still being a master of none. This makes it a little difficult to identify just a few traits for a successful entrepreneur but here's the six sub-zones of the Entrepreneurial Zone.

INNOVATION

It goes without question that an entrepreneur has to innovate. They are the inventors of the new world we have yet to enjoy. Every single mod con we possess came about from the innovation of earlier entrepreneurs. Such inventiveness is in the DNA of human beings.

So we could use a stick as a weapon or make that same stick into an axle for a wheel. The common trait used in such innovation is our ability to forge new things from components which had a different initial purpose.

When the tree first grew that stick, it had no idea whether bits of it might be used to kill or maim, or to transport someone from A to B. The entrepreneur saw differently.

OPTIMISM

Entrepreneurs have to be intrinsic optimists. They have to look on the bright side, not only for their products or services, but also for the benefits their prospective clients will get from doing business with them.

Some entrepreneurs who are setting out to change the world will be optimistic for society as a whole. Some may be carrying batons for all life on the planet. Some may even be thinking about colonising other worlds.

TENACITY

Such optimism can make entrepreneurs into masters at failing. They hone the ability to pick themselves up again and start over. Where others would have given up, they just keep going. Some reckless entrepreneurs bet their savings, their home and their relationships on their dreams.

Of course, this trait can also be seen as pigheadedness, blindness and even foolhardiness.

VISION

Their tenacious nature attunes entrepreneurs to opportunity where others may see adversity. They love shining light into dark corners where others fear to tread. They look at what's under the metaphorical carpet while others sweep things they would rather not see under it.

Entrepreneurs also possess '20:20 foresight'. They see the future, while many are struggling with the present or, even worse, are crippled by the past. Entrepreneurs see the whole vision in split seconds. They are adept at tuning into light bulb moments. When we see light bulb moments as potentially being 'future memories', it puts the entrepreneur's real talent into perspective.

So there is something very subtle again buried deep inside an entrepreneur's DNA. They are are seers and timelords.
They are mindful of the past, learning from their mistakes and experiences. They can also see clearly right into the most wondrous future. Furthermore, they don't let the past bring them down or wallow in self pity. Neither do they get carried away by a future that hasn't happened quite yet, spending their fortune before it has amassed.

NAIVETY

One of the traits of those who aren't entrepreneurial by nature is fear. They might be fearful of failing or being ridiculed.

They might even be fearful of being successful and, as a result, being placed in the spotlight. The press love to build someone up and also to report on their fall. This stereotype gets engrained in our collective consciousness and can stop thousands of people from shining their light.

Consequently two of the essential charms of many entrepreneurs are naivety and innocence. By not seeing potential pitfalls, the associated fears don't come to the surface. If they knew what was to befall them, some entrepreneurs wouldn't have got out of bed in the first place. This of course is the polar opposite of vision.

LUCK

The most successful entrepreneurs are focussed on doing exactly the right things, in the right order, right now.
They also turn up at the right place and meet just the right people at the right time.

There is something very special going on in the minds of an entrepreneur. Recently, scientists using MRI scanners have noticed neurons in our guts firing 5 to 10 seconds ahead of a stimulus in real time. Note it's now also known that we have more neurons in our gut than cats do in their brains. This accumulation of neurons is known as our enteric mind.

We've all regretted not going with our gut feelings at some time or other.

It turns out that our gut mind is an active centre with a primitive consciousness and awareness and that it is in continual communication with our brains. It somehow knows things before we do.

ZONING IN

We can think of an entrepreneur who trusts their gut as being an ultrapreneur. Their secret to the ease with which they generate ideas, and make things happen, is their ability to always be a few seconds ahead of everyone else. When an ultrapreneur is on fire, everyone else is playing catch up.

Ultrapreneur (noun): an entrepreneur who is way ahead of the pack. [Derivation: ultra- (Latin: beyond) and -preneur (French : prendre, to take)]

The term ultrapreneur is much more appropriate to describe an entrepreneur who is at the top of their game. These are the people that are not so much 'under-taking' something but 'over-taking' others. Ultrapreneurs are not so much occupying the Entrepreneurial Zone but defining what this zone is in the first place. They are across all the sub-zones and invent entirely new zones of their own making.

To ultrapreneurs, the concept of a boundary is simply not entertained. If something can be done, it will be done. They will either do it themselves or they will know someone who can make it happen for them.

[6]

The Creative Zone

WHILE THE LIVE PERFORMER HAS THE ADVANTAGE OF THAT ADRENALIN RUSH TO PUSH THEM TO NEW HEIGHTS, FOR THE MOST PART, THE CREATIVE PERFORMER WORKS OFF LINE ON THEIR ART, THEIR MUSIC OR THEIR WORDS.

The motivation for writing that book or composing that new song can prove elusive. Artists all too often find their creative juices run dry. An external deadline, or perhaps an author's advance, can provide an incentive but it can also be a curse.

When we are in flow however, it's almost like we have been taken over by an external force and we are just an agent and co-collaborator in the creative process. Time takes on an ethereal quality and whatever we produce can be near perfect first time around.

It may becoming clear that the boundaries between the zones is not hard or even fixed. Creatives need to be masters of the Time Zones. Any artist should be superbly creative about hopping around the zones, including some Danger Zones.

Entrepreneurs and performers need to be comfortable in the Creative Zone. All of them will want to get their audience and customers into the Happy Zone - and to keep them there. As a self-serving example, the very writing of this book requires me to enter the mind set of people in each of these zones.

The key to managing creative process is to recognise that there is not one zone but several. Anyone involved with a creative task has to work through a number of steps to ensure their work gets finished. If they are in the wrong mode at the wrong time, their work can end up on a slush pile of their own making.

Any half-written manuscript or part completed canvas is a sign that the creative process has hit a road block at one of the sub-zones. Indeed before even embarking on a piece of work, we need to have the entrepreneurial vision to be able to see it through and the persistence of a live performer to make it happen. Again this indicates how zones cross-fertilise each other.

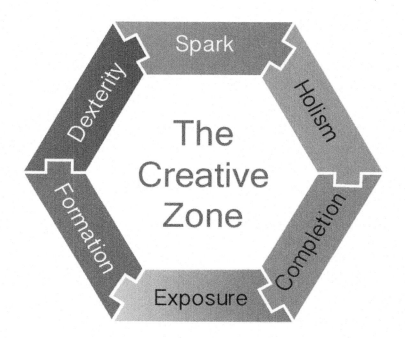

SPARK

This is when the seed idea arrives that wakes you up with excitement in the early hours of the morning. For many artists, such sparks fly in all by themselves.

The artist doesn't have to wait for that light bulb moment to turn up. It is possible to enter this sub-zone under their own volition by meditating daily. This doesn't mean having to sit cross-legged in a cave humming "Om". Just taking a walk in nature, and especially near water, for 10 minutes a day is a great practice to adopt. City dwellers can normally find a park or open space. When out walking it's a good idea to look up not down, as that activates the more creative areas in the neurology.

If you can't fit a walk into your day, meditation machines and smartphone applications are available that induce the state for sparks to fly in. Some of these can be used to get us into the zone our eyes open.

Alternatively, if you have never meditated before or you have trouble getting your mind to go quiet, you'll find resources at the end of this book to help you get into the zone.

HOLISM

Often along with the spark, we see the whole vision for the project. An author might see a series of books. A photographer might capture one scene that leads to a series of shots. A composer may get a whole symphony from one bar of music.

Apocryphally, Isaac Newton got the whole theory of gravity in less than a split second but then took the rest of his life to document it all and work out the maths.

When we are fortunate enough to have such a high level vision, it can help us focus on assembling the component parts of our art in a sensible order. At any time our creative juices run dry in the process, all we have to do is flip back to the sub-zone of the Spark to get a new seed idea to unblock the flow.

My personal tool of choice to help us generate and perceive 'whole-ism' is the mind map. It allows our right brain to hold the complete vision while the left brain concerns itself filling in the detail.

Of course, this is gross simplification for how our mind actually works. Note too that just doodling around a theme or meme can generate a similar result.

DEXTERITY

What makes the difference between an artist in flow and one that struggles is the flair that they have for their craft. Some are naturally blessed and predisposed to their art; others have to work a little harder at it.

Like any live performer, the artist works best when they become unconsciously competent about their craft. Practice, as always, makes perfect. When an artist doesn't have to worry or think about the mechanics, they can then bring flair, deftness and finesse to their work.

FORMATION

When we see a finished sculpture or listen to an opera, we tend to initially perceive the whole. The artist who brought it into the world however knows every detail of the piece. They know how the shape of a body was built on a wire former, or that a particular chord was built from a specific triad of notes.

Having constructed the whole, they are able to explain to an interviewer what their motivation was and how it all came about.

Successful artists are also required to be fabulous project managers. They must manage building blocks such as words, notes or clay. They also have to control the providers of external services, such as book cover designers, picture framers or sound mixers. The ability to keep many plates spinning may also be required across multiple projects running concurrently.

COMPLETION

Knowing when to stop is the key trait of a successful artist. It helps of course if their whole vision is clear and they have managed the production process well. It also helps to have a goal that puts completion of the project high on their To Do list.

To set this goal, when you are meditating or out walking, rather than musing about the creative project per se, think about what completion of it would mean to you. Imagine what doors will open for you, your family and your business or career. Think about what effect your art might have on people who enjoy it and what they might be inspired to do a result.

EXPOSURE

Many artists are not natural live performers. When it comes to shouting about their work and their talent, they would find it easier to have an agent.

I always say to authors I work with that their edited manuscript gets them 25% of the way there, and that when they publish they are about 50% of the way there.

The remaining 50% of the task requires them to tell the world about their work. We are required to become show offs and expose our heart, mind and soul to all and sundry. For some, this can mean we enter one of the Danger Zones, typically the Fear Zone. Indeed, this can bring us full circle as the very thought of entering that Fear Zone can dampen that initial creative spark.

For those that are naturally shy, these days the Internet allows us to be reasonably faceless and to promote our work without actually meeting people at all. Those natural show offs should be wary though as nobody likes anyone who shouts too loud about how brilliant they are.

ZONING IN

Creativity is something that tends to ooze from the pores of an artist when in the zone. The creative process doesn't stop with the production of the work but also in its promotion.

What is well known is that, like any muscle, if we don't use an aspect of our neurology, it atrophies. I know from experience that the best way for an author to promote their first book is to write book two. The best way to promote book two is to write book three ... and so on. At the same time you grow your portfolio, you also grow in experience.

There is another benefit from living and breathing in the Creative Zone. You tend to meet, and hang out with, others of a similarly creative persuasion. This has the great benefit of making it not so much of a lonely and solitary place to be.

[7]

The Learning Zone

ONE TRAIT THAT ALL THE INHABITANTS OF THE DOING ZONES SHARE IS THAT THEY ARE ALL QUICK LEARNERS.

Anyone who wins an Olympic gold has learned something a bit special in order to get them to the top of that podium ahead of their rivals. Entrepreneurs are continually learning from both their successes and failures. Many artists hone their craft until their last breath.

For many people though, the very idea of learning brings back horrible memories of their school days and having to memorise an unending stream of seemingly useless information. For many an adult then, the idea of voluntarily entering the Learning Zone can result in fast entry to one of the Danger Zones.

We might enter the Fear Zone thinking we might make a fool of ourselves. If we don't pick it up as fast as everyone else, this can tip us straight into the Anger Zone, both with ourselves and the teacher.

It's a great shame that the thought of learning something new brings up so many demons as, when delivered and approached in the right way, learning can be a lot of fun. Indeed, it could well be that one of the purposes of our life and time on this planet is for us to learn. If you think about it, we are even hard wired to learn. Our very survival is based on it.

Early humans had to learn to hunt to survive. As a baby, we learn to make sounds so that we can tell our mother when we are hungry or uncomfortable. We learn things nowadays so that we can get a job, so we get paid, so that we can afford to eat. Nothing has changed that much apart from, as a species, we have learned an incredible amount since we came down from the trees.

A quick random browse around a web site like Wikipedia will tell you that collectively humans know quite a bit today. At the same time, there is a near infinity of unknown information we could each still learn. We know for a fact that we know so many more things than our grandparents and great-grandparents. It is a reasonable assumption therefore that our descendants could know a lot more than we do. That said, sitting on our laurels and remaining in our comfort zone can feel much safer than going out into new and uncharted territory. As a result, many people stop learning at the earliest opportunity.

To enter the sub-zones of learning, we need to be incentivised. So just imagine, for starters, that you could 'earn more' if you 'learned more'. What then would life be like if it could be easier, not harder? Could it be possible we could discover the meaning of Life, the Universe and Everything?

INQUIRY

We are inquisitive by nature and this is the starting point for all learning. It appears that we arrive on planet Earth un-programmed and as a blank sheet of paper. We can't feed ourselves, bathe ourselves or look after ourselves in any way.

Slowly we acquire communication skills followed by a level of self-awareness. When we enter our teens and through to early adulthood, we strive to learn what it's all about and find our place in the scheme of things.

It is this fundamental desire for many people that drives us to ask questions, to look under stones to see what's there and to look up at the stars and ask questions like, "Are we alone?".

INSIGHT

Bearing in mind there is a near infinity of things to know, it could be a bit tricky to know what to learn. Should it be to play piano or to learn how to fly a plane?

The trick to knowing where to direct our inquisitiveness is insight. To better understand the subtlety of how this works, it's better to express this quality as 'inner-sight'. When our attention is drawn to something, it is almost like an external force is guiding us. If we are attracted by something, or possess a natural propensity to it, we should follow this with all vigour. What then happens is that we get put in a position to learn more and more. As a result, our level of expertise and competence rises accordingly. Note that this is healthy so long as you are not in a Danger Zone, such as one of addiction.

Furthermore, if you feel resistance to learning, then this can be one of the positive attributes of the Fear Zone. It may be a sign from the 'early warning system' of our gut mind that something is not quite right for us at that particular time.

ABSORPTION

When it comes to learning, it's not just our brains that get in on the act.

Our neurology extends over our whole body and our muscles. Even our internal biochemistry learns and responds to the world around us.

If you learn to play a musical instrument, when you become proficient, your muscles just know what to do. The way that vaccinations work is that antibodies learn how to fight infections. Learning anything new is an aspect of our consciousness. Learning a physical action is part of our body's awareness and learning at a cellular level is part of our intrinsic nature. We are hard wired to absorb learnings.

At the same time, there is no real theoretical limit to how much we can learn. You can learn as many languages as you like and take on board as many facts as you like. It's only a myth that learning is age dependent.

This myth contributes to collective belief that un-absorption in old age is inevitable.

CONTEXT

Some people revel in learning purely for learning's sake. Being able to remember a seemingly unending list of unrelated facts for a pub quiz can be fun, and even useful if you win. Learning out of context though is ultimately fruitless.

There has to be a point. It's also harder to learn and recall pure facts than it is to be able to work things out from first principles.

What is of much more value is understanding how all the nuggets of information fit together. When we forge a connection from one fact to another, it also forges a permanent connection between them in our neurology. This allows us to learn a seed fact and a rule that connects it to other related facts. So if we know 2+2=4 and 4+4=8, this allows us to know 'without knowing' that 4444+4444=8888 without having to do the maths.

PURPOSE

Armed with this new mathematical knowledge, we can reach greater insights and perform bigger sums like 4,444,444+4,444,444=8,888,888. But what can we do with these gems of extrapolated wisdom?

Well by way of example, back in the late 1970's, some smart people learned how to do clever things with digital electronics. They worked out how to design and build digital calculators.

These innovative devices used basic mathematical rules to allow us to perform amazing arithmetical calculations in seconds. Previously they would have taken ages to carry out on paper in long hand. Having learned how to make machines that can add, subtract, multiply and divide, a whole new semiconductor industry then came about that lead to the personal computer revolution.

If you have a mobile phone, you have a computer many times more sophisticated than the one that landed man on the Moon.

The so-called digital revolution is a practical application of learning to build bigger and more complex tools based on what we learn.

What's more, from such feats of technical wizardry comes even more potential for learning. The computer revolution has resulted in an exponential leap in inter-communication. More and more people can swap notes.

More and more data can be correlated and analysed. We have eyes and ears in orbit around our planet that we can use to see how our world is doing and how we might be affecting it to both its benefit and detriment.

As far as we know, this places us in unique position. Perhaps unlike any other species, we can now learn how to shape our own destiny and evolution. That constitutes a pretty big purpose!

HUMILITY

With knowledge can come much power. To put things in context, humanity represents the tiniest fraction of the biomass on the planet and we have been around for the briefest blink of a cosmic eye. When people talk about extinction of life on the planet, they mostly mean the extinction of human life. If we were to disappear, as may have happened in the past, the Earth would not miss us that much. It has bounced back from many mass extinctions already and we know one could happen at any time in the future.

With this in mind, it's prudent to be humble about our place in the overall scheme of things and to use our learning wisely. This means we have to cherish both our amazing technology and the magic of our self awareness. At the same time, we should marvel and protect the smallest algae upon which our whole food chain is based. We must help just the right amount of sunlight to reach the surface and ensure the air is clear and fresh. We must nurture, not rape, the planet's natural resources.

The genie of what we know should not be put back in the box. Any knowledge and learning we accrue has to be used wisely, ethically and ecologically.

ZONING IN

By just being alive, we cannot help but learn. To learn nothing is something we actually have to work hard at doing. Learning though is something which is much easier to do when we have an incentive. It's even easier still when it's enjoyable.

Like all muscles, the more we learn, the easier it is to take on new learning. Each new learning forges new neural connections and, if you need a good incentive, it's thought to offset the onset of dementia.

With this in mind, what is not to like about learning?

[8]

The Time Zone

TIME IS NOWHERE NEAR FIXED AS IS THOUGHT. IN FACT, THE MANNER IN WHICH WE THINK EVEN AFFECTS THE PASSAGE OF TIME.

For starters, not many people realise that the normal human mind is only capable of having one thought at a time. Just think about what you are thinking right now and notice how the thought about what you are thinking replaces what you are thinking about. You may want to read that last sentence again!

This means that if you are worrying about something in the future or mulling over past events, you will lose focus on what is happening right now. This means that for much of their waking day most people are around 33% efficient.

I am sure you've heard the phrase, "If you want something done, give it to a busy person".

This works because 'busy people' are often masters of focus.

On the other hand though being able to instantly recall past events, and to zoom ahead to events yet to pass, tells us something remarkable about ourselves. We all possess a powerful Time Machine called "our mind". More specifically, it's called "our minds".

In general, when we are in any of the Doing or Beings Zones, time often takes on a different quality where we can get two or more hours work done in less than an hour. It's almost like the task at hand gets done in whatever time is available. Woe betide anyone who breaks your concentration when you are in the bubble of your personal Time Zone.

Neuroscientists are discovering remarkable things about the brain and our neurology. Firstly, they can't readily find a clock in our bodies. It appears though that our left brain, rather than being the centre of logic, monitors the passage of time and holds the sequence of events. Our right brain seems to be 'everywhen' else.

These discoveries can be made by anaesthetising areas of the brain in healthy patients while awake and then observing their perception of time.

What's more remarkable though is that other parts of our bodies seem to run to different time clocks completely. Our gut mind seems to produce a stimulus seconds ahead of an event occurring in real time. It seems to be running ahead of time by up to 10 seconds. It also appears to be a guide and alarm system for events we should be aware of to ensure our safety and well-being.

The speed of our breath too seems to regulate and interact with our perception of time. Breathe faster and time speeds up; slow your breathing down and time elongates almost in inverse proportion. It's even possible that the speed of your breath could affect your longevity. The giant tortoise breathes around 4 times every minute and lives to around 140 years. Elephants live for around 80 years and breathe around 8 times every minute. Most humans however breathe around 12-15 times a minute and our pre-industrial revolution life span was around 50 to 60 years.

So what seems remarkable about the Time Zone is that we have more control over it than we might first think. Using simple breathing techniques borrowed from yoga, we can slow down the perceived passage of time so we can get more done in less elapsed linear time. This even works in group environments.

By tuning into our gut mind, we can save hours by noticing coincidences, signs and serendipities. Our gut can also save us time by preventing us from making the wrong decisions.

What is perhaps even stranger still is that when we enter the Chillout Zone, we can even tune into 'future memories'. This allows us to take leaps forward in creativity that could take us days or weeks to otherwise deliver. Many scientific discoveries are made in this manner. Luminaries like Archimedes, da Vinci and Newton were adept at tuning into such moments of prescience.

Once we take ownership of the passage of time, we become timelords who are masters of qualities of the sub-zones of time.

PATIENCE

When we get anxious about time, we can become impatient. This can lead us to rush into things or to fret or worry if we, or someone else, are late. Bearing in mind we can only have one thought at a time, worrying about time is actually a waste of time.

A kettle we watch boiling seems to take longer solely because we are focussed on the passage of time, as opposed to any other thought stream. If we try and force events outside their natural course, we restrict ourselves and put unnecessary pressure on the timelines.

PUNCTUALITY

Perhaps conversely, if we are not mindful and respectful of time when it comes to others, this also distorts timelines out of their natural shape. Fortunately, when you exit the Danger Zones and occupy the Being Zones, you will find you are never late for anything.

I am never angry if an author comes to see me for mentoring if they are running behind time. It just tells me that personal time management is one of the issues we need to deal with. Simply spotting this, even without speaking to the client, of course saves a bit of time in our session. In passing, I have noticed that people who don't wear watches uncannily always seem to be on time.

PERCEPTION

When it comes to our creativity, one of the biggest time bandits are our own thought processes. When our internal and external chatter is loudest, we will be at our least productive.

Just try and write something when you are also trying to think about it to experience this phenomenon. When we pause during writing, it's so we can stop to think. When we write, the thinking abates and it's like someone is reading to us.

Being perceptive about our state of mind is a crucial step in allowing us to take control of our time

MALLEABILITY

Time seems to bend depending on how we are thinking. If we are stuck waiting around with nothing to do, time stretches. If we are active, time zooms by. So we can take control of it by being mindful of it.

We should be malleable to events that seem to throw us of course and appear to steal our time away. Counterintuitively, by tackling some events out of what we think is the natural and logical sequence, we can get things done more quickly. When we are in the Being Zone, it seems there is an external agency pulling our strings.

PRESCIENCE

Because we live in a world with a forward arrow of time, we can remember events that have past, to some degree or other. It is illogical, and perhaps a bit crazy, to countenance that we all possess an ability to experience 'future memories'.

It is known though that our gut mind works ahead of our conscious awareness so this could explain 'near-field' precognition. This is possibly how you sense the phone is about to ring and know, a second or two in advance, who is on the other end.

If we open up to the notion that our 'future self' has information which is useful to us, we can then pick up amazing insights. By tuning into such 'future memories', we can save ourselves buckets of time.

Note that there's a self-limiting time logic that means the lottery results are off limits, unless of course we are already destined to win.

SYNCHRONISM

By far the best way to truly become a master of the Time Zone is to tune into natural time. A combination of our man-made calendar, incandescent light bulbs and central heating insulates us from many of the excesses of the seasons.

We are each predisposed to be more creative at different times of the day and different seasons in the year. If you go back over past projects and map which were most successful and easy, you will quickly find correlations with the clock and calendar and your productivity.

It pays great dividends too to pay attention to the phases of the Moon as these have an influence on our creativity.

We can of course be creative at any time of day or night and productive in any month of the year. By noticing and working with natural rhythms, we learn to go with the flow of time and to stop pushing it back uphill.

ZONING IN

So while we may not be able to reverse the arrow of time, the flow and passage of time can be warped, bent and manipulated. We can change our relationship with it such that tasks fit easily into the time available.

By being mindful of our thoughts and the manner in which we think, we can stretch our perception of elapsed time. Quite simply, we can get more done in less time.

When you take up permanent residence of the Magic Zone, you save even more time still. In this special zone, serendipity abounds and everything you need just seems to turn up with minimal effort, just at the time you need it.

This of course helps us save bags of time!

[9]

The Decision Zone

ENTREPRENEURS, ARTISTS AND PERFORMERS WHO REACH THE PINNACLE ALL DID SO BY MAKING GOOD DECISIONS, AT JUST THE RIGHT TIME.

Some may well have had decisions made for them. An agent might well have got them a deal or a gig that shot them into the spotlight. Many an entrepreneur finds their niche after being made redundant. We know that the decisions we make today influence all our tomorrows.

Now our senses are bombarded by billions of bits of information every second, while the normal human conscious mind is only capable of holding one thought at a time.

Thankfully many life dependent processes work autonomously. Most of the time our body decides our heart and breathing rates for us. Our blood chemistry is a fantastically complex, self-regulating system.

Our unconscious mind too is continually scanning for nuggets of information that may be of use to us.

If you are talking to someone in a crowded, noisy room and if someone else mentions your name in an adjacent conversation, you will often pick it out.

So with this huge difference in data rates between our unconscious and conscious processes, how do we ever hope make any decisions?

Some people seem to consistently make the wrong choices. They can be unlucky in love and life. Others seem to never put a foot wrong and land on their feet all the time. Is there perhaps a lucky 'decision' gene that some are blessed with?

Let's take a simple choice between two options as an example.

Let's say you are in a new town and out looking for somewhere good to eat. You come to a T-junction and don't know whether to turn left or right. There seems to be lights and activity both ways. Unbeknown to you, to the left lies a group of muggers and to the right there is a restaurant with fabulous food and a special offer of a free starter.

Incidentally, when I 'chose' this example out of all the millions of possible illustrations, I had no idea if it was strong enough, or even relevant, as an example to support the brief explanations below. I just worked on trust.

Nowadays of course, we can look up information ahead of time and check out restaurant reviews on the Internet. We could always ask a passer-by. This glut of terabytes of daily increasing information can also lead to overload and indecision.

Often though we have to rely on our intuition and gut instinct. Only after the event will we pick up enough 20:20 hindsight to know if we made the right call.

Fortunately when it comes to making a decision we have not one but three cognitive processing centres. The secret to getting them in alignment leads us to the place where we rarely put a foot wrong and good fortune comes into our world as a result.

The obvious decision making centre we possess is our brain. Our brains are bilateral in function, with the two hemispheres processing information slightly differently. As mentioned, for most people our right outer cortex sees the whole vision. In our example above, it will see there are two choices to be made. The left outer cortex will be checking for details. It will process smells wafting on the breeze. It will decipher sounds that could indicate a lurking group of aggressive youths, or plates clanking and cutlery clinking.

Classically and obviously the signals feeding our main organ of awareness are our main senses of sight, hearing, smell, taste and touch.

At a lower more subtle level, two other mind centres operate silently on our behalf. Our heart centre informs us if it likes or even loves the 'look' of one direction over an other. Our gut mind informs us about the safety of one course of action over another. Remember that these two mind centres also operate a few seconds ahead of our conscious mind.

These centres are what the animal kingdom use and rely on constantly for survival. They are still active in humans but quite often overridden by the loudness of the chatter in our conscious mind. If you ever hear yourself say, "I wish I'd trusted my gut or followed my heart", then you have witnessed that override in operation.

So it pays dividends to reconnect and strengthen these connections if they have atrophied somewhat. The key to doing this is to take a tour around the sub-zones.

CONSISTENCY

When faced with two choices such as turning left or right or saying yes or no, we could always just choose one over another. So at all unknown T-junctions, we could choose that we always make a right turn. This means we have a good chance of being correct about 50% of the time.

Most often though we make such choices based on other conditional parameters to better stack the odds in our favour. If looking for that restaurant, we could go towards brighter lights. We might choose to go downhill so that, after we have eaten, we can burn off an extra calorie or two walking back up it.

Such consistency allows us to take a course of action, measure it's efficacy and subsequently to repeat it if it works, or to modify our algorithm accordingly if it doesn't.

CONGRUENCE

When we learn a new fact or skill, after a time and some repetition, it gets committed to our memory. What is happening internally is new neural pathways are being forged so we don't have to consciously remember how to do it again. It will just come naturally.

When we expand this model to the neural connections between our head, heart and gut minds, the more we make good decisions, the easier it becomes to be more right than wrong. When head, heart and gut are in alignment, we become unstoppable and near infallible. In some ways, our gut and heart are older and wiser minds. While they may not be independently self-aware, they know a thing or two and should be listened to.

SERENDIPITY

Of course, when we hit that T-junction, we could always just flip a coin and let fate take us either left or right. If you were do to this all the time, this is actually a consistent behaviour which is also quite congruent.

The real art to living a serendipitous existence is knowing what signs are significant and what represent pure noise.

Conveniently, this is where the next three sub-zones kick in. I should point out here that I listed these sub-zones as they occurred to me without giving any consideration to how they flowed together. Now I am expanding upon each one, the sequence I 'chose at random' has a beautiful, flowing logic - in my 'minds' at least. That's serendipity in action.

SELECTIVITY

So let's say we turned right on a flip of a coin but then found a row of 10 restaurants, which all looked equally fantastic. We have landed on our feet for sure but now have ended up being overwhelmed by even more choices. If there were just two restaurants, another flip of that coin could be used.

We are unlikely to be able to eat more than one full meal so the next choice we make is crucial. So we use our past experience to filter the possibilities open to us based on what we have liked before. We combine the output of this filter with the input of what we fancy right now. We should also consider too where we want to end up as a result of eating that meal. Our brains are brilliant at such selection but there is another more subtle way to filter.

If we ask our gut mind a question, it will respond internally and almost silently with a "Yes" or a "No". Try it now by asking your gut mind if this statement is true. So we can interrogate our gut mind as the first level of selection.

Let's say this leaves us with 3 out of the 10 restaurants to choose from as our gut mind rejected 7 of them. We can then consult with our heart mind and also internally ask its opinion. While the primitive gut mind generates either that "Yes" or a "No", the heart signals its status in the form of a level. So it's either cold, luke warm or hot about things. If you ask it for a rating for each restaurant, you will zone in quickly on the optimal selection.

Note that if you repeat this exercise on a different day, the results may be completely different. Our gut and heart minds tune into to signals beneath our awareness all the time and act as our silent guides and guardians, if we let them. They may know of future serendipitous events that may unfold as a result of choosing one restaurant over another.

DILIGENCE

Many people faced with too much choice either err on side of caution or do some analysis. You might look at all the menus and compare prices or look in each restaurant to see which are empty and which are full.

If too empty, this tells us something and if too full, it might take ages to get served.

A smart move would be to casually ask a diner leaving a restaurant that you like the look of if they enjoyed their meal.

ACCEPTANCE

At some point in the future exists a version of you which knows exactly which restaurant to choose. This could be because that 'future you' experienced either a good or a bad meal. Now while we live in a world with a forward arrow of time, there is nothing in physics that states explicitly that we cannot tap into future memories.

This allows us to play a trick on our mind and our imagination that can produce extraordinary results. It works for more than just choosing a restaurant of course. We can simply let the decision arrive.

If we ask our imaginary future self for a sign, one will arrive as if by magic. For example, you could ask for an indicator of where to dine, such as the restaurant from which the next diner leaves. Alternatively, you could label them one through to ten and then notice when you next see a corresponding digit on a car number plate. Numerology is a powerful guide when you learn its keys.

Zoning In

Now I hope you are not more confused about making decisions at the end of this chapter than at the beginning. When we get to the end of this book and explore the Magic Zone, my aim is for any clouds to lift and for veils to part. Let me leave you with two notions for now that might at first sound paradoxical.

First, one model of our world is that we live our lives backwards but experience them forwards.

Second, it is a paradox of our existence that everything is preordained while we still have free will to change absolutely anything.

You can now of course make a decision to ignore both statements and dismiss them as bunkum. If you take this latter view, you may also decide to read no further.

You may also decide to find out why these statements might not be as paradoxical as they first seem.

If you need a carrot to help you read on, it is simply this. Each of us has one simple decision to make. We can choose to live a life that is hard and to continually push water uphill. Alternatively, we can walk in grace and ease and go with the flow.

DANGER ZONES ARE WHERE WE COME OFF THE RAILS.

THEY ARE WHERE LIFE GETS TOUGH.

THEY ARE WHERE THE WORLD SEEMS OUT TO GET US.

THEY ARE WHERE WE SUFFER UNDULY.

THEY ARE WHERE WE BLAME OTHERS.

THEY MAKE US QUESTION THE POINT OF EVERYTHING.

[10]

The Negative Zone

YOU MAY HAVE HEARD THE ADAGE THAT IT TAKES SOMETHING LIKE 43 MUSCLES TO FROWN BUT ONLY 17 MUSCLES TO SMILE, SO WE SHOULD ALL SMILE BECAUSE IT'S EASIER.

Well this is a bit of an urban myth as not everyone uses the same muscles in exactly the same way, or to the same extent, when smiling or frowning. Some people can express their displeasure by subtly raising an eyebrow; others can 'smile' with the minutest twinkle in their eye. Like all muscle groups too, they tend to set in the mode they are most comfortable and accustomed to. This might make it harder for naturally happy people to exhibit displeasure and for those with a cross to bear to manage a grin.

Some people seem to be predisposed to negativity. To my knowledge, no specific study has been carried out to see if optimists consume less energy than pessimists. It is intuitive though that the those with an inclement outlook in life seem to be the people who have a harder time of it.

They tend to be more prone to illness and it's probable that their longevity is affected as a result. As with the chicken and the egg, sometimes it's not clear what came first and if the external misfortune preceded the negative, internal demeanour.

Like all traits, there is undoubtedly both a genetic component as well as an element which comes from nurture during upbringing and education. As for all the zones, they are infectious and this can apply both positively and negatively. We cannot help but infect those around us with our moods and it's hard not to get sucked into another's way of being.

In the Danger Zones, the sub-zones do not so much represent different attributes of each zone. Rather they show scales, degrees or even shades of that particular zone. At one end of the spectrum, we might be slightly irritated. At the other, we could become outwardly destructive to both ourselves and others.

So we might start in a relatively mild 'Zone of Low', or a 'Zone of No', only to end up in an angst-ridden 'Zone of Woe'.

By grading the sub-zones in this manner, we can see how easy it is for something trivial to get blown out of all proportion.

In regression therapy in particular, often by dealing with the most trivial of trigger events, fundamental changes can be made in even the most extremes of behaviour.

At the end of each of these Danger Zones, you will find some help to 'zone out' from its influence. This gives a possible route back from the more unhealthy aspects of any particular zone.

You will also see later how Danger Zones can be nullified by surrounding them with zones brimming with positivity.

Let's take some tentative steps into the grades of the Negative Zone. This zone is a breeding ground for the seeds of the other Danger Zones to germinate. If you spend too much time swamped in negativity, you can easily end up wallowing in more than one of these unhealthier zones.

Pessimism

I am always amused by the saying, "An optimist is a pessimist not in possession of all the facts." Pessimists do tend to over-think a situation and therefore can be incredibly intelligent and quite creative. They will easily be able to come up with a raft of ideas not to do something. Often they are right too and love to tell you that they told you so.

Where they miss out though is in having all that fun from trying. You will never win a lottery if you don't enter and similarly, in life, you have to be in it to win it. When pessimism blurs into pragmatism it can be a good thing. It is though an attitude and position from which we don't move forward and we don't learn, even if it is from our mistakes.

DISCONNECTION

A negative stance and outlook can be something that we pick up at an early age. If a child is not included in play, they can easily become an outsider and quite lonely as a result. You can see how easily a pessimist can be bred in the playground. Indeed groups of such like minded children may even form cliques. Some will find solace and comradeship nowadays in online forums and in the back waters of the social media world.

The antidote is to enfranchise, to engage and to love the pessimist. We must embrace them for who and what they are, not who they have been.

NIHILISM

When a pessimist finds themselves on the outside of society, their condition can become entrenched. Nihilism is like a positive and purposeful pessimism which manifests in permanent negative action. Nihilists don't tend to be born but made by events and experiences in their lives. This gives hope as anything that can be made can be remade or unmade.

Helping a nihilist change their spots is a tough act. They will twist any positives you send them into more negatives. You can invoke the cunning of the double negative and have some fun by telling them not-not to do something. More constructively, a spell in the Kindness or Loving Zones might generate better and more long lasting results.

STUBBORNNESS

This is actually a low level fear that results in obstinacy. On the surface, a stubborn person appears to be negative but dig a little deeper and you will often find a fear lurking.

When the root cause of the fear is found and dealt with, you will be amazed at the speed with which their stubbornness softens. If they are a bit of a nihilist too, it's a bonus if they can be lead to this revelation themselves.

RESISTANCE

Sometimes people will put up barriers and resist all reasonable suggestions to change their behaviour and stance. I am sure many therapists have had at least one client who resists all treatment.

When this happens, whether in a therapeutic context or in life in general, it's important to respect the free will of the 'resistee'. If someone doesn't want to change, it is somewhat arrogant to make them.

Behind any such resistance there maybe a deep-seated stubbornness serving to protect the person. Unlike the merely stubborn person, if someone is resistant to change, it could well be that its simply not a good time to make that change. Sometimes we have to let events play out in their own good time. Our intuition should be the guide here as to whether intervention is really needed, and if so when.

FUTILITY

If we spend too much time dwelling in negativity, there can come a time when we simply give up on everything. For some, this might mean eschewing company and society in general.

Others may seek a more terminal solution. We can see people who are suicidal as giving a cry for help. Sometimes though, people want to stop the world and get 'off the bus'. Some may believe in heaven, hell or reincarnation and see such drastic action as a reset for their soul. Some may be suffering from terminal conditions and want to choose the time and conditions of their own departure from their mortal coil.

This sub-zone is included for completeness only and not because I have any answers. It should be remembered too that while externally the situation might look futile, the person suffering from it may be seeing it in a positive light and as a release.

ZONING OUT

It might be logical to assume people in the Negative Zone exude some sort of negative energy, which obviously can be picked up by others. The term 'negative energy' is a bit of a misnomer.

If you think about it, all energy is something which is not zero. So it's more accurate, and helpful, to think of it as 'positive energy' pointing in the wrong direction.

Relabeling it as such gives us a clue how to get out of this zone by reframing the actions, and redirecting the attention, of someone stuck in it.

So if someone thinks the world is against them, we could ask, "What have they got against the world?".

If adversity visits their door, they could explore what they can learn about dealing with such misfortune. The best antidote for a negative is simply a positive.

For more severe cases of negativity, and indeed Danger Zones in general, an exploration of the Healing Zone can pay great dividends.

[11]

The Anger Zone

ANGER IS A WEIRD AND POWERFUL FORCE.

Like gravity, we know it exists and that it is extremely pervasive. We can feel its significant external influence but nobody can see it. It only exists initially in the mind of the angry person but it has a long lasting reach that can spread like wild fire.

Anger too has its shades and degrees, starting with disgruntlement and ending up in out and out violence. We have to treat anger with kid gloves. It can be healthy to vent it. If we bottle it up, the pressure cooker can blow. Clearly a strategy for anger management would be useful.

Sometimes it's impossible to prevent yourself from being angry, even from the most trivial of causes. Perhaps someone pushes in front of you in a queue. So what if you have to wait a little longer to get served? Perhaps the other person pushed in front of you unintentionally or had something going on in their life that had put them into another Danger Zone.

So what if you see something on the news that makes your blood boil? If someone had injured someone else, what is needed is compassion not anger. Getting enraged only pours more fuel on the fire of the root causes of the problem.

Now of course, that's really easy to say, or to write, but when it comes to managing our anger, it can be a constant battle to keep calm, requiring almost constant vigilance on our part. For example, you may well be quite good at managing your internal state should transgressions be made against you. If one of your loved ones gets crossed however, you can all too easily get very angry on their behalf.

To complicate things still further, repressed anger can dramatically affect our health and well-being. It's quite possible that depression, and even some cancers and strokes, are seeded by bottling things up.

Fortunately though, anger can be easily neutralised and transmuted by slipping into either a Doing or Being Zone. So if something makes you flip your lid, why not slide into the Creative Zone and do something about it?

For example, I wrote a complaining letter, but in humorous rhyme, to an airline recently only because they had changed my preferred seat allocation on the plane. Note that the cause of the anger was trivial in the extreme and I only got angry as my partner was disgruntled. Imagine my surprise when I received an apologetic, funny poem in response and when a bottle of champagne arrived a few weeks later. This was like a 'First Class Upgrade' straight to the Happy Zone.

This is a classic example of how better results can be achieved simply by moving to a zone with more positivity. If someone crossed a boundary, perhaps it's a disguised cry for your help. Showing some kindness and cutting a little slack is the most fantastic and rapid way to turn a transgressor into an ally. The alternative is that the most insignificant of issues takes you into ever deeper and darker sub-zones of anger.

IRRITATION

Anger is often seeded by mild irritation. If we are disgruntled or peeved about the world in general and wallowing in the Negative Zone, then the most minor of irritants can set us off. This gives a clue that anger is not a real force at all but something that can arise from nowhere in those that are so predisposed to rise to the bait.

In a similar way, some people have a peanut allergy that needs just a few molecules to waft past their nose to send them into anaphylactic shock. The solution is not to ban all peanuts but to discover the biochemical, or even psychological, triggers and then to learn how to deal with them.

By dealing with the root cause of irritation, the likelihood that it will ever reoccur is reduced greatly. If it does surface, you then have a coping strategy in place to deal with it.

RESENTMENT

When we respond to continual irritations, resentment can set in all too quickly. At this point, we can even sense the seeds and signs that the irritation is about to start and we zero in on them instead.

So rather than being angry at the irritation, we transfer our anger to its purveyor. If you like, we could call them "the irritator". Previously we may have said, "That makes me angry". When we are resentful, we change our comment, whether expressed internally or externally to, "You make me angry".

ANNOYANCE

At the point when we generally 'lose it', we also lose the objectivity. If someone or something out there is annoying to us, we rarely think that the real issue here is that we have let ourselves become annoyed.

Let's say you are reading these sentences and getting a bit vexed, it's all too easy to shoot the messenger. I don't mind telling you that it took me ages to write this chapter as I kept thinking about all the things that had annoyed me in the past. I ended getting grumpy about my own chapter in a book of my own making.

For all I know, I am conjuring up similar memories for you and you are getting grumpy at me for reminding you about them. How annoying is all of that for both of us?

LIVID

So if we don't snip irritations in the bud and vent our spleen, we can end up going ballistic. This can cause us to react in an uncharacteristic manner which we may end up regretting later. What happens here is something potentially more insidious again.

So something annoyed us that made us act out of character and do or say something that we later regretted. We get doubly angry at the source of irritation and at ourselves. We then get a bit entrenched and want the other side to apologise first ... and so it goes. You can see how things can get out of hand and how wars can start from simple misunderstandings and differences of opinion.

VENGEFUL

So just four sub-zones in and how's your blood pressure? Well, there's a couple of levels of anger to go yet I'm afraid.

When someone won't apologise for making us angry, thoughts of revenge sneak in to allow us to set the world to right. An eye for an eye is called for and you are the person to dispense justice, assuming you haven't just called in a lawyer.

We can even get quite creative about how sweet the revenge might be. Many a wronged partner has cut holes in clothes or put dead fish under floor boards.

Woe betide anyone who dares to mention the possibility of taking a trip to the Loving Zone. This is the place to go when such vengeful thoughts surface but few people are capable of rising above the situation. When a grieving parent forgives their child's killer, people can even get angry about that.

PSYCHOSIS

If we let anger fester and grow, it becomes dangerous and harmful, much like a cancer. The most insignificant triggers can instantly lead to irrational behaviour completely out of kilter with the level of response.

When psychosis sets in, people get hurt. This is when things have gone too far and there is no easy route back. This is possibly why some mass murderers kill themselves as their last act of anger.

ZONING OUT

When anger kicks in, we are allowing our innate animal nature to take over from our logical persona. If we let it go too far, feuds will start either internally in our heads or externally with our transgressors and enemies. If we hurt someone else, we are only hurting ourselves.

So when anger visits, the first course of action is to nip it in the bud at the earliest opportunity. If you slip into the livid zone though, it's time for drastic action. So take a breather, sleep on it and slide over to the Creative Zone and work out how all parties can kiss, make up and apologise.

For vengeful and psychotic behaviour, external intervention is probably the only recourse. Traditionally pharmaceuticals may temporarily suppress and manage the behaviour, noting that self administered drugs or alcohol will just fan the flames. What can produce amazing results though is skillful and professional mediation and group work.

With perspective comes 20:20 hindsight which may lead to the ability to simply brush the source of irritation away. What then happens is that the things and people that used to annoy us seem to magically vanish from our world.

[12]

The Sadness Zone

THE WORST THING YOU CAN DO TO SOMEONE WHO IS SAD IS TO TELL THEM TO SNAP OUT OF IT, OR THAT THINGS COULD BE WORSE.

As far as someone who is sad is concerned, things are pretty bad and they may not take kindly to platitudes. At the same time, we don't want to leave people to wallow in self-pity and despondency.

As for all the Danger Zones, it pays dividends to be aware of the source of the sadness. Obviously, the passing of a loved one or a pet is enough to cause anyone to feel sad. In these cases, the natural grieving process is necessary and should be allowed to run its course. Transiting the Sadness Zone, at some time or other, is a necessary facet of life.

People who spend time in the Negative Zone can tend to be a bit gloomy by nature, unless they use sarcasm as a form of entertainment. Several comedians make great use of this type of persona for example.

In general, most people are sad about something, or sad about their lot in life, at some time or other.

Sadness takes on a more insidious form when it morphs into depression. Many people deal with depression by resorting to alcohol or various legal and not-so-legal highs, like amphetamine. Some get their highs with the adrenalin rush from dangerous sports. The chance their sport might be life threatening and offer a release is part of the complexity of this dis-ease.

Depression can also have a biochemical cause which is often counteracted with a barrage of anti-chemicals, turning peoples' bodies into a hormonal battle ground. Seasons, nutrition and even the amount of daylight we receive may also play a part. Seasonally Affected Disorder [SAD] is one of the most appropriate acronyms that there is.

The reason sadness is so debilitating is that it affects our heart and gets us right at the core. This can make it impossible to be creative while you are sad. That said, many an artist has painted their way both in and out of depression. Composers even have the minor key as their natural tool of choice in order to emote their sadness and then to evoke it in others. If you want to write a sad poem, or a chapter about sadness like this, it helps if you think of sad times. Expressing our sadness through our art can often be marvellously cathartic.

So sadness and loss go hand in hand and often lead us into other Danger Zones. If you are ever burgled, you'll be both sad and angry about it.

If your partner leaves you, this can make you sad. If they leave you and go out with someone else, all sorts of chemical reactions ensue. If you find out they were seeing someone else while still going out with you, you may lose the sadness but end up in the livid or even the vengeful sub-zone of anger.

Many spurned loved ones end up turning to alcohol or drugs to console themselves. Accordingly, the Addiction Zone is also the Sadness Zone's bedfellow.

Of all the Danger Zones, it's perhaps the one that can so quickly send us on a downward spiral that it's hard to extricate ourselves from. A journey through its sub-zones shows how layers of sadness can so easily weigh us down.

Unhappiness

Our sadness may just be a malaise where we just aren't happy with things. If you are a creative or an entrepreneur, you may be sad about the way things have turned out after all your hard work. The simplest way to quickly reverse out of a miserable state like this is to list all the positives.

Despite things not working out, think about what you have learned. If you have to try again, be creative about what parameters and conditions you can change next time to get a completely different outcome.

MELANCHOLY

There are unhealthy energies floating around the world. Some of them inhabit buildings and places. Specifically low lying regions and basins with hills either side are places to avoid if you have melancholic tendencies. Latitudes with reduced sunlight during the year are no go areas too. If you work in an office, the building or air might be sick.

I have first hand experience of negative energies and entities that are akin to the Dementors of Harry Potter. There are people who can help clear these from you if that's what you feel is occurring. Note that whether these may be real or imagined, they seem to be attracted by sadness.

A great practical first step is to find a healthier place for you to be, even it's just for a holiday and some respite. So run for the hills, get some fresh air and bathe in some sunlight.

DEJECTION

Dejection is a byproduct of rejection. If nobody loves us, we can quickly stop loving ourselves. When we enter this sub-zone, you can see how the slope downwards can get steeper and more perilous. What makes this sub-zone worse is that the more dejected we become, the more we erect a barrier around us preventing people who might help from getting near us. If the help is pitiful in nature, this can only make things worse.

A great way to deal with dejection is to take in a change of scenery.

Taking up a new sport, or learning a new skill, can get us out of a rut and allows us to mingle with new people. We may be dejected about our capabilities in one area only to find our niche was right in front of our noses, or at least just around the corner.

GRIEF

When we suffer a loss we can become inconsolable. It may sound passé but time is the healer here. If this makes sense and is true, we can capitalise on the interrelationship with time and our consciousness to help.

If we are stuck in a waiting room with nothing to read waiting for an appointment, time drags interminably. If we have a weekend away in a new place with new sights and sounds, time flies by. This gives us the clue to a possible solution, bearing in mind that it may not be appropriate to party and we have to let grief takes it course. By keeping a grieving person busy and engaged and their mind occupied, we help speed up the linear passage of time. The grief will still take time to diminish but it can be helped on its way.

HEARTBREAK

When loss is very severe it affects our physiology. Many people who suffer from a figurative broken heart end up having a real heart attack or other circulatory problems, like hardened arteries. This can even happen when people retire or get made redundant.

The idea that we are not loved can quite literally be a killer. So, if you find yourself in this sub-zone, you will find the Kindness and Loving Zones a place to find some comfort.

DEPRESSION

If you spend any length of time in any of the preceding sub-zones, you can very easily end up being depressed. Depression can be triggered by anger, specifically when anger is not expressed. There are many types of therapy to help with depression ranging from the mild, with techniques like tapping [EFT], to the severe like Electro-Shock Therapy [ECT]. It's been experienced in some cases that depression can even be lifted merely by giving the 'shock' that ECT might be administered so that no real shocks need be applied.

There is a more subtle and more permanent solution to helping people out of depression though and that is to give them purpose. When we enter the Chillout Zone, we find a new way of being and a new sense of what it's all about. Chilling out and meditating is not about retreating out of society and hiding in a cave. It gives us space and time to work out how and when to engage and what it is we are here for.

ZONING OUT

Many people look for meaning and an external cause and solution to sadness. Perhaps they have brought it on themselves and there's some kind of karmic retribution in operation. Some indeed will be drawn to religion for solace, while others might shun their god for forsaking them.

Thankfulness is by far the best cure. So try to be thankful for all the things you have as opposed to all the things you may have lost. Know too that, in the fullness of time, some context will appear to help the sadness dissipate. While one partner, or opportunity, may have left you, it could be only because an even better one is about to appear in your life.

Second best to thankfulness is to spoil yourself and to go on a break which I like to call a 're-treat' or a 'me-treat'. This of course gives you something to be thankful for.

Thirdly, any activity which helps to quieten the mind will also help quell the demons that haunt us. Combining all three of these techniques is of course a great option.

The Guilt Zone

GUILT COMES AT US FROM TWO DIRECTIONS. IT CAN BE EXTERNALLY APPLIED OR INTERNALLY GENERATED. THE FORMER KIND OF GUILT LEADS TO THE LATTER.

Externally applied guilt comes from the collective. It comes historically from religions, governments and the legal profession and latterly from the media and even from competitive sports.

We have laws and rules to keep us on the safe and narrow. We are introduced to them from an early age and throughout our schooling. We are told what we should 'not' do. These rules are often phrased in the negative. For example, seven of the ten commandments include a "shalt not". In the classroom, and many homes around the world, we can imagine exasperated teachers or parents shouting, "Don't do that". These admonishments might be echoed back negatively with, "No" or "Shan't".

Many lawyers make fortunes from assigning and ascribing guilt. The news media predominately report on the negative aspects of our society. Many journalists are continually on the hunt for the guilty party and scapegoat.

In sport, if a team loses, the manager can be heard in the post match interview coming up with all sorts of excuses to save his job. Rarely do you hear them say that the other team was simply better than them, or how exciting and how much fun the game was. So much emphasis is on winning these days, not taking part. The losers can feel guilty simply as a result of not winning. We live in a culture of blame where everything has to be someone else's fault.

So what chance does a child have but to grow up with some aspect of guilt when they are surrounded by it? Some churches even use the concept of original sin as a central tenet of their dogma. This means that an innocent baby has sinned before they have a chance to take their first breath. I remember being a relatively good boy, not so much so I would have a chance to go to heaven, but so that I wouldn't go to hell. If I though I sinned in some way, I would agonise about even the most minor of transgressions for days afterwards. I know some of this entrenched and embedded guilt affects my behaviour fifty years later.

When we have done something against the law of the land and it can be proven that we did so, we are labelled as being "Guilty" or "the guilty party". We even have to 'plead guilty' as if we are begging for forgiveness.

For some people transgressions can become habit and misconduct a way of life. Their moral compass has lost any connection with the 'True North of Righteousness'. They don't even suffer from guilt and may act from a position of their own self-righteousness, which may be way out of kilter with mainstream society. Indeed they will often operate in clandestine, guilt-free groups where lawlessness is the norm.

While those outside the group may see them as being 'sin-full', they will consider themselves as 'sin-less'. Some of them will be revolutionaries, some even terrorists. Only history will later decide who were the heroes and which were the villains.

As for all the Danger Zones, there are shades and degrees of guilt.

DISGRACE

This first level of guilt is relatively easy to extricate ourselves from with a simple apology. If we disgrace ourselves in some way, we can say we're sorry and admit we have made an error. If we do it quickly enough, ideally before our guilt is discovered by another party, we may even get off lightly.

Many politicians use this tactic and re-emerge on the scene quietly when one of their peers is the subject of another day's bad news. Not only is no harm really done if we genuinely learn from the incident, but it may open the door for us to rise in our standing.

INDISCRETION

While we may disgrace ourselves inadvertently or misguidedly, we can be more consciously indiscrete. Here we may perform an act knowing it is wrong but hoping or assuming we won't get caught out.

If we are not found out, the guilt can lay with us and plague us for years, perhaps unconsciously. If our indiscretion is uncovered, our ability to be trusted takes a knock. Again, apologies are in order but also a positive act to right the wrong may be needed. In cases of law for example, this could be some community service rather than a custodial sentence.

REGRET

When we perform an act which we feel guilty about, we may impose a more insidious penalty on ourselves. The regret we pick up from our guilt can live with us forever. The smallest incident that reminds us of what we have done, even years later, is enough to throw us right back to that time when we sinned.

I remember all too well a practical joke backfiring that I performed on the happy couple at their wedding around 30 years ago. Guess what now comes straight to my mind every time I attend any wedding many years later. Rather than being happy for the new couple, if I slip into reverie during the service or reception, I am reminded of my impetuous foolhardiness.

Even though I was forgiven at the time and it was seen as a prank that misfired, this particular 'sentence' will be with me for life.

FAULT

When we are at fault and know we are guilty, only two options are normally open to us.

We can admit our guilt and take the rap. By serving our penance as soon as possible, we give the guilt the earliest chance to be cancelled out. Alternatively, we can hope we never get found out in which case the guilt can stay with us and operate silently.

There is a third alternative. If we don't feel we can admit we were at fault, we can change our behaviour and our ways. If this is the chosen route, a spell in the Kindness Zone is a great tonic. It can help both us and any people that our indiscretions may have affected.

TRANSGRESSION

When we really overstep the mark, performing a kindness might not be enough to make good for our deceit. If peoples' property or even their lives have been damaged or stolen from them, laws have been broken. It's then time to 'pay the price'.

Reparations, not just platitudes, are in order. The words used here are quite informative.

We have pay 'damages' or serve a 'sentence'. This implies we have 'damaged' someone or something and that a 'sentence' saying we're sorry must be spoken by us continually while we are locked away behind bars, or for the rest of our lives.

MISCONDUCT

Some people get up each morning with the intent to do wrong. They may even be quite entrepreneurial about their activities and quite creative about covering their tracks.

They have created a Super Zone using qualities from the Entrepreneurial, Creative and Addiction Zones. If they ever get found out and serve their time, they may even write a book and see their exploits on the silver screen.

At the time they commit their misconduct, we may chastise and blame them. We may though watch their film as a guilty pleasure, secretly wishing we could brave enough to be so naughty.

ZONING OUT

Any counteraction of feelings of guilt has to be dealt with from both a personal and a group perspective.

First, we must forgive ourselves for any transgressions we still carry with us. A spell in the Learning Zone is what's needed. Moving forward, if you inhabit the Being Zones, you will find that the circumstances where you could be guilty of anything tend to vaporise.

Next, guilt at a societal level has to be addressed. Religions would be more popular if they came into the twenty-first century, dropping all fear-based dogma and fully embracing the Loving Zone. While many purport and strive to work from a position of love, a close look and revision of underlying doctrine is overdue in many cases.

The legal system and the media could both benefit from a period of introspection and a phase of revolution. People really should be innocent until proven guilty, not clandestinely branded as guilty before the fact.

[14]

The Addiction Zone

MANY ADDICTIONS START OFF AS ROUTINES AND THE FIRST LEVEL OF ADDICTION CAN BE RELATIVELY HARMLESS OR EVEN BENEFICIAL.

So for example, I wrote each of these chapters immediately after morning meditation and before answering emails. This is a habit I find hard to break nowadays so you could say that I am addicted to doing it this way.

If I can't fit my morning meditation into the day, I have even been known to get grumpy and slide into the Anger Zone. In general though, I hope this is an example of a healthy addiction. If this practice made me forget to take the children to school, or to put out the recycling, you can see how easily an addiction can slide downhill and have negative consequences.

A good example a relatively modern addiction is a craving for social media. You may even see some people checking their Twitter feed and Facebook Wall on their mobile phones while they are walking along. It is all too easy to take the high ground and get moralistic about this habitual behaviour.

Someone might be monitoring a social media campaign to raise money for a charity, or sending a message to a loved one. Others might be wallowing in negativity, or even hate, and be creating a virtual Negative Zone, dragging others into it in the process.

One person's drug dependency might be someone else's life line. Cannabis can be used both as a relaxant and a pain killer for cancer sufferers. An addictive gambler might have been sucked into their habit as a last ditch attempt to feed their family. When that plan fails, a visit to a pay day loan company might be next on the list.

Sexual addictions can be a hidden cry for a love of another form. Like all addictions, the chemical cocktails released in the body generate a corresponding 'inner drug' addiction. What hope is there for someone so afflicted? We are biochemical beings after all and sometimes we just can't help ourselves.

It's clear there is a fine line between habit and addiction. Classically we label it as the latter when it has an adverse affect on ourselves and others. Like all learnings and behaviours that we adopt, addictions forge patterns in our neural networks both in our brain and our body. This gives all addicts hope as our neurology can be rewired in an instant with the right treatment.

The reverse is also true and a trip through the sub-zones tells the story of how innocuous behaviour can swiftly lead to disastrous consequences.

INCLINATION

Addiction starts with a hook. We get to like something which might even be a guilty pleasure. Again this is how the zones so easily morph into each other to create bigger zones.

Geneticists, psychologists and sociologists will have their views on where the seed inclination comes from. The tendency these days is to point the finger of blame at genes, education or society.

All such inclinations ultimately come from within as most addictions start with a perceived need, which often boils down to a lack of love.

We may be missing love coming to us from someone else or, more commonly, suffering from a lack of self-love. This is the seed that causes us to look elsewhere for our fix.

CRAVING

We know addictions are taking hold when the cravings kick in. It then becomes so much harder to break the habit. When we focus on the lack of something or other and cannot get it out of our mind, we are hooked.

Our neurology is driving us towards satisfying our addiction and nothing can get it out of our mind. Here's where a spell in the Chillout Zone can come in handy. When we learn to quieten our mind, we become free from the tyranny of our own thought stream. This gives us both a quick exit route out of the Addiction Zone but also a 'Free Pass' with which to enter the Magic Zone.

Many people who have successfully managed their addiction use mindfulness techniques. When they learn the magical nature of what can be done, they turn from addict to teacher. This shows the real magic of the mind.

DEPENDENCE

If the healthy and essentially free route of controlling our 'monkey mind' is not taken or overlooked as an option, dependence on our addiction can quickly take hold.

Our biochemistry and neurology becomes hard wired such that our addiction becomes integral with our nature.

The addiction becomes part of our day and we feel out of kilter if it's not satisfied. For mild or healthy addictions, this isn't so much of a concern so long as it doesn't escalate. If however the addiction is harmful to us or others, we are on a slippery slope.

OBSESSION

When dependence slides into obsession what happens is that an addiction isn't just a facet of our day, it becomes our day. Some people might have to have a cigarette or a drink as soon as they get up and before they brush their teeth or have breakfast. No amount of internal or externally applied logic will help.

Even powerful mind mastery will struggle against the addictive need as often the obsessive person will have applied a cunning logic to justify their actions. They make stories up in their heads that make it OK to be addicted.

ENSLAVEMENT

A further degradation overtakes the addict when their behaviour is controlled by the addiction. As mentioned, these days it could be as innocent as having to check emails before you go to sleep or when you get up.

When this happens, we also enter the Fear Zone. We worry about what will happen to us and what we might do if our source of addiction is removed.

Enslavement requires a master and a servant. When addiction was a mere inclination or craving, we were the master and the addiction served a need and made us feel better. When the addiction becomes the master, it's time to seek help.

SELF-DESTRUCTION

All too often we hear of a celebrity who cannot handle the pressure of being in the spotlight. They resort to a self-destructive mix of drugs, alcohol and adrenalin rushes. Sometimes these fixes come along with the life style; sometimes they are needed simply to cope with the life style.

In some ways, each person on the planet is a celebrity. Just being human, being alive and incarnate is an amazing feat. It takes much fortitude to sustain ourselves and not to crumble under the pressure of living from day to day.

Modern society has ushered in amazing benefits and delights, while also being a jungle for some who find day to day survival a real struggle. As a result, some find solace in taking themselves out of the loop. At this point, the addiction can become self-terminal.

Zoning Out

For the milder forms of addiction, a spell in the Chillout, Kindness and Loving Zones may be the best remedy.

When addictions become more severe, external help is needed. As for some of the other Danger Zones, there are many therapies and therapists that can help. Some people will benefit from the chemical approach, others from hypnotherapy and the like. Some will have to go right to the edge, stare at their own oblivion and then return from the brink.

As always, learnings are to be made. Ex-addicts make by far the best counsellors for others so afflicted. There is always light at the end of every tunnel.

[15]

The Fear Zone

FEARS ARE GENERALLY A GOOD THING. THEY KEEP US SAFE AND SOMETIMES EVEN KEEP US ALIVE.

They emanate typically from the lower mind centres like our gut. As mentioned when we explored the Time and Decision Zones, this means such fears also operate slightly ahead of our conscious mind, acting like an early warning system.

We become fearful when something can potentially harm us. So we are right to be afraid of a venomous snake, or even a wasp. When in the Danger Zones though, some fears can have a detrimental effect. They can be imagined, self limiting and even irrational. If you suffer from triskaidekaphobia for example, no amount of common sense can convince you that the number 13 isn't evil incarnate and out to get you.

As for all the Danger Zones, there is a balance. Some daredevils that are fear-less can be seen as foolhardy. The adrenalin rush from their exploits drags them into the Addiction Zone where they need a bigger and bigger 'hit' - sometime literally!

As for all the zones, fears are infectious. Many are picked up in childhood from our elders. Simply blaming others for our fears though could allow us to slide into the Anger Zone. If a parent or teacher either intentionally or unwittingly installed a fear in us, they may have done it with their best intent in mind. They may only have wanted to protect us. Sometimes though, what happens is they were infected by the fear themselves. So rather than expressing anger towards them, we should feel compassion for their affliction.

At the same time, if you are a parent or teacher, you should be mindful of the two types of fear that children can pick up quickly - namely the fear of ridicule and the fear of the unknown. Many a poor essay or average performance in a school play can dampen the creative spirit for life. The fear of all things unknown, and trying things because they are different, can similarly crush a child's natural curiosity and their desire to learn.

Fortunately, when we overcome a fear, quite often we can feel slightly silly that we ever let it affect us in quite the way it did.

There are some fears though that don't express themselves clearly.

When I began to help authors break through their writer's block, it became clear to me very quickly that there was always an underlying cause to their procrastination. I know this all too well as I was similarly afflicted. In pretty much all cases, the writer's block was a symptom not a cause.

If you think about it, it is illogical for us to procrastinate from doing something that is not only potentially enjoyable but that can also improve our lot in the world, like writing and publishing a book. This book for example, and all the doors it is opening, came about solely from the publishing of earlier works. My life now is dramatically different from how it was before I first had my name on the cover of a book. Yet I remember taking ages to get around to publishing my second book. Instead, I ended up helping loads of other people get their books published ahead of me.

The reason was simply this. The two times in my life when I had been most financially successful in my earlier career coincided with the times I had been most stressed. So unconsciously I had associated stress with success and my procrastination was actually masking a fear of success.

When I did finally get around to publishing my second book, the floodgates opened and at least one book a year started popping out almost effortlessly. Success at last you might think but sadly book sales were a trickle not a flood as another fear was lurking in the shadows, the fear of failure.

Whether an author gets a publishing deal or independently publishes their book, for the most part these days book promotion is down to them. Rather than promoting my earlier works, and potentially failing, I would simply avoid the very notion of a failed book promotional campaign by throwing myself full tilt into the next book. After all, if you don't try, you can never fail.

I make no apologies for some of this chapter being about my personal journey. By sharing where I am, and where I have come from, my aim is to resonate and empathise, not to preach or brag.

Tackling such fears is often more like a continual process rather than an arrival at a specific destination. This is because fears are multi-layered. We get over one hang up only to find another we have to tackle. When we wander into the sub-zones of fear therefore, it becomes clear how small seedlings can grow into dark, inescapable forests.

CONCERN

Fears start out very innocuously. They can even remain buried for years before circumstances bring them to the surface. When they do poke their heads out, they sometimes just appear as a slight concern. You feel somewhere in your water that something isn't quite right or that the wheels are about to come off the bus.

When this happens, it's a good idea not to ignore any signs and to sweep them under the carpet, as they may resurface later with more vehemence. Neither should you act unduly or out of character. Keeping a diary or a journal can be a good way of keeping a track on them as sometimes they operate seasonally.

FOREBODING

A foreboding is a stronger form of a concern. If you ever get up one morning and don't feel right, it's worth being vigilant for the day ahead. Again, don't panic as this can make things worse, just be observant.

When these portents darken our door, and we get a feeling of precognition about them, this is actually quite a good sign. It shows you are tuned in. Many ignore such signs and events can overtake them and get out of control. So when a feeling of dread visits your door, respect it but don't be fearful or you will just feed it. Going for that walk in nature near water will help. Incidentally, if the fear subsides as a result of such a simple act, you are well set for entry into the Magic Zone.

ALARM

When alarm kicks in, your concern and foreboding are confirmed. You were right, something is amiss and you need to react. Or do you? There is only a small step from the alarm sub-zone to the next shades of fear so, if anything can be done at this point, it could be beneficial.

When a fire alarm goes off in a building, you should quite rightly evacuate and leave it to professional firemen, who are the experts. When an alarm goes off in your life then actually you are the best placed expert to deal with it. It's time to take action to quench the metaphorical spark that caused the alarm to flare up in the first place.

So think about what you are alarmed about for starters, and what you can do to put out the fire. Do you need to apologise or back track? If you wander into the Anger Zone, this will only pour fuel on the flames. An even more counterintuitive reaction to alarm is to make a beeline to the Loving or Kindness Zones. This is a tactic that needs some practice and skill to pull off, which is analogous to learning how to smother a burning fat fryer with a wet towel.

Panic

If you don't manage to smother the flame of alarm with your conscious mind, our irrational, lower level brain kicks in to protect us. This is where we either fight or take flight. Sometimes of course, if the situation is life threatening, this is the right course of action.

Irrational panic though is a destructive force and can suck people around us into our drama. The simple technique to offset the onset of panic is to take conscious control over our breath. By taking several deep belly breaths, where we really use the diaphragm, we can calm ourselves or anyone else down. What also happens is that time elongates so you have more chance to react to what ever is causing the panic to occur.

Terror

There are times when we experience a physical reaction to something that is terrifying. A poisonous snake or spider is a real threat.

A ghost that goes bump in the night may be real or imaginary. A wide open space is real enough and terrifying to an agoraphobic but imaginary to most people.

So if something is really terrifying, then a reaction is a good thing. If it's imaginary, it is time to seek help

PHOBIA

Another good time to seek help is for an imaginary phobia. So, for example, when a large furry moth comes anywhere near me, my better half is right to tell me to get a grip. My moth phobia does not bother me that much, and actually provides a source of amusement to others, so I'm living with it.

If however you find yourself irrationally panicking over something trivial, there are many fast and safe therapies around. Hypnosis, regression or tapping all have their place and a Google search will uncover someone who can help locally. Many of these therapies can also be delivered remotely over the phone or, ideally, using Internet video conferencing.

ZONING OUT

The best way to counter fears is to embrace them and to even thank them for coming to your attention so that you can evolve and move on.

The next best technique to quell fears is to take small steps to put your head above the parapet. When you find you don't get shot down, you can show the world more and more of your talent. Quickly you will discover a world that is not out to get you, but one that actually welcomes what you have to share.

If your fear level is more severe though, get help as soon as possible.

In general, Danger Zones are not so much to be avoided. They are places we can learn and grow. By travelling through them, and coming out the other side, we find ourselves able to slide gracefully into the Being Zones. Here's where the Danger Zones can fade into becoming a distant memory.

BEING ZONES ARE WHERE WE FIND
PEACE AND TRANQUILITY.

THEY ARE WHERE WE FIND PURPOSE.

THEY ARE WHERE WE BECOME LUCKY.

THEY ARE WHERE WE GO WITH THE FLOW.

THEY ARE WHERE LIFE BECOMES EASY.

THEY ARE WHERE WE FIND OUT WHY WE CAME TO BE.

[16]

The Healing Zone

WHEN WE THINK OF A HEALING ZONE, WE MIGHT THINK OF IT AS BEING A PLACE LIKE A HOSPITAL OR A CLINIC. FOR SURE, THESE ARE ALL PHYSICAL ZONES WHERE SOME HEALING UNDOUBTEDLY TAKES PLACE.

The real healing zone is slightly more ethereal and intangible than any doctor's surgery. It is a place in our minds and bodies where we go to in order for healing to take place. It's a place where we have to take full responsibility for our own well-being.

This particular Healing Zone is purposely situated at the exit of the Danger Zones in this book and at the start of the Being Zones. Indeed, it's a place to take stock before moving to a new way of being.

If we are unwell, it's natural we seek pity and want some comfort, either from another human being or in the form of a pill or a sticking plaster.

It pays dividends though for us to ponder if there is a ulterior purpose for any feeling of dis-ease.

Perhaps we are burning the candle at both ends and it's nature's way of getting us to slow down. Perhaps we are consuming too much of one thing or not enough of something else. Perhaps we are living and working in a toxic environment. Such toxicity could be physical or mental.

There is no question that many illnesses are seeded from a thought or state of mind. For example, eating disorders such as obesity and anorexia could be rooted in lack of self-love or poor self-worth. This signifies both a cry for help and a cry for health.

So the real Healing Zone is a place we go in our minds.

First, if we are taken ill, we should take that recourse to get ourselves back on track. It's not a good idea to let things fester, just in case they get worse and become irreversible. Whether we favour traditional or complementary medicine, we should go and see that expert who can look at our condition and prescribe something, or some course of action, that will get us better.

The next step though is to change the conditions that caused the illness in the first place so that it doesn't visit our door again. This might be a change in lifestyle or even a change in job. It might mean that we should hang around with different people. Whether it be a common cold or a bad habit, many diseases are contagious and infectious. Even the bad luck that gives rise to accidents is something that can be caught.

Such a change in lifestyle allows us to enter a special zone indeed. In this zone, disease simply doesn't exist. We keep illness at bay more often that it crosses our path.

On the rare occasions when we do succumb, we see benefit and a message in anything that is sent to plague us and darken our door.

Wellness is often represented by an equilateral triangle where mind, body and spirit are in harmony. This is a pretty accurate metaphor and one that all health practitioners would do well to utilise, with both themselves and their patients or clients.

What is of more importance is that our health is not the responsibility of the government, the health service, the newspapers or the media. We are responsible for maintaining the balance of our own triangle of well-being. Our mind can upset our body or our body can dampen our spirit. Our spirit however, even though somewhat intangible, can support our body and enrich our mind. This leads us to the essential aspects of the Healing Zone.

ENERGY

It is the conventional view that our energy comes primarily from what we eat and drink. While this is undoubtedly important, what we can get from an energy drink or energy bar is somewhat insignificant compared to the true source of energy available to us all.

Our breath is a key provider of power and energy to our body and our mind. If you feel yourself flagging during the day, just breathe deeply five or so times, really using your diaphragm, and you will give yourself a nice boost. You can even do this ahead of any creative task to pump-prime your system. Sunlight too provides us with free energy, so long as it's not over done.

CARE

We can of course take too much energy on board and even have too much of a good thing. It's vital that we are care-full and don't get care-less. Should the cabin depressurise on an aircraft, you are told to don your own mask first so that you can better help others. This approach is also applicable to our health.

In the same way that disease can spread, good health has the effect of being catchable. This is especially true when applied to mindset. Care over what we think and what thoughts we transmit is key to healthy living. When we take care, we are so much better placed to give care.

CENTRING

If we are off balance and our triangle of health is skewed, it puts strain on all those around us. All too often the carer suffers as much as the one being cared for. The carer's needs are so often unrecognised.

What has happened in these circumstances is that the person who is ill has de-stabilised loved ones with their illness. This doesn't mean the other people have caught the same disease but that their well-being has taken a knock. This is even more reason for us to be totally responsible for our own health and balance.

OBJECTIVITY

When we are truly in the Healing Zone, we see all disease as a symptom of something that is underlying. Each of us is the sum of all our past timelines and our current state of health can be affected by any or all events that have gone before. Years of early over indulgence or abuse can catch up with us later in life. The sum of any negative thought patterns take a toll on our body.

So if you are a health professional, or just self-diagnosing, it's important to look at underlying causes for any imbalance. The dis-ease that is presented may not be what is needed to be treated.

NURTURE

Our sense of well-being is something that also needs care and attention. A plant needs water, nutrients and sunlight to grow. We have to cultivate a similarly healthy environment for us to live in. This will also involve an amount of weeding as, if we live in a cluttered and noisy environment, it can make it hard for new shoots to thrive.

We should also be mindful about the variations over seasons. It makes sense to stock up for winter and to spring forward for the summer months. In the same way, we can prepare for good health in our later years by the actions we take today.

RELEASE

Seeing our health as our own responsibility brings a huge amount of release. By taking ownership ourselves, we take the burden of responsibility from all the health professionals. Sure they can still provide care, but we must work with them to get ourselves back on track. By being in the loop, healing speeds up and our illness has minimal affect on others. When this is scaled up, we get release at a macroscopic level such that society as a whole becomes healthier.

So by freeing ourselves of our own dis-ease by owning up to its source, the collective is released too and we enter a positive spiral which everyone benefits from. By adopting this new stance, we release ourselves from the illusion we are enchained and everything is the fault of someone else.

ZONING IN

So this form of Healing Zone is a bridge from those Danger Zones into a new way to run our lives. Here's where a huge shift in thinking must occur.

Our good health is not the responsibility of our doctors, our healthcare system or any government. It lies with each and everyone of us. The prime factors affecting our health are our lifestyle and mind set. If you are unfortunate enough to be unwell, the road back to good health is largely down to you.

Of course, we can get help from both traditional and complementary medical practitioners. They can mend broken parts and give our bodies a service if needed. When you fully engage with the Being Zones however, your reliance on others to ensure your own well-being diminishes.

[17]

The Kindness Zone

A KINDNESS IS MUCH MORE THAN AN ODD TOKEN GESTURE THAT MAKES US FEEL GOOD. BEING KIND TO BOTH OURSELVES AND OTHERS IS A VIABLE AND WORKABLE LIFE STRATEGY.

As for happiness, much evidence is emerging that any positive action benefits our biochemistry and hence our well-being. To some extent, this is an important byproduct.

What is of much more significance is how our actions bounce back on us. Any kindness we perform will get reflected back to us, but magnified. This does not mean that we should be kind to others for a selfish, ulterior reason. Any such karmic subterfuge will only trip us up unexpectedly down the line.

Adopting a kindness strategy is much more fundamental than performing the odd kindness in the hope people might think nicely of you.

Taking a more holistic approach to kindness has more far reaching implications for our lives.

For starters, when we perform acts of kindness, any reflected kindness does not necessarily come back directly from the person or people you have been kind to. More often, it comes from someone who may have absolutely no connection with any party involved with the initial act of kindness. Note that there is no angelic 'bookkeeper' recording all our good and bad deeds in some sort of cosmic ledger.

The 'payback' may come at the most unexpected time too, sometimes years after the event. It might even happen before the event occurs, such is the magical nature of the kindness effect. Experientially, it appears that kindnesses multiply. One act of kindness will generate many more in return. So we need to take a step back and a step up in developing and executing any strategy.

Ask yourself a simple question. Do you want to live in a cruel or a kind world? Also ask yourself if you tend to wait for others to take action before you follow their lead. Surely something as fundamental as making kindness a central tenet for our society should be adopted at a governmental level. It would save the tax payer billions after all in so many areas.

Well this would be great but it takes years to change a single law, not months and certainly not days. We can all instigate our individual kindness strategy today and start reaping benefits by tomorrow. Kindness multiplies and is beautifully infectious. The quicker you perform a kindness, the quicker it bounces back at you. At the same time, the people you are kind to will then be kinder to other people they meet.

Your kindness has a massive ripple effect which is where the amplification comes from. They don't even have to have read this book, such is the power of positive intent.

As you go about your days, open doors for people, let other drivers out from side roads in traffic, or just smile. Everyone you do this to will repeat that act to at least one other person. Just imagine this spreading throughout drivers in the rush hour. Traffic jams might even reduce if everyone cut a bit of slack to others.

This leads to to another perhaps counterintuitive phenomenon. We can also be kind to ourselves. So long as that kindness is not at the expense of others, a little self-indulgence also works a treat.

Let's say you're reading this book and can't wait to get out in the world to kick off your kindness initiative. So get to the end of this short chapter and go and give yourself a treat.

You should then follow this with the other magic trick that should be done every time a kindness is bestowed on you and that's to say "Thank you". Sometimes too kindness will arrive at your door serendipitously. This means you won't readily be able to identify its source. When this happens, that silent and internal "Thank you" works a treat.

The sub-zones of kindness give us further illumination into the magical nature of a simple act of kindness.

RANDOM

Performing at least one act of kindness a day is all that's needed for this whole strategy to work. As they can be a short as smiling at that stranger or holding that door open; there is no need to give up your day job.

What works best though is if you do them randomly. So be kind at different times of the day to different people. Also flip into the Creative Zone and be inventive about the kindnesses you bestow. What of course happens then is that the kindnesses that come back to you will exceed your wildest dreams.

MEASURED

Being kind does not mean giving all your hard earned cash away. The best kindnesses are those that cost you absolutely nothing than a little of your time, but that have a huge impact for others.

When new contacts come in from social networks, I randomly ask some of them what I can do for them that will take me no more than a minute, but that will really make their week. Some come back with the most trivial requests which take no effort at all on my part. Some have answered saying just to have had the offer has made their week already. Then no further action on my part is even needed. Many also ask my permission to use that strategy on others. This is the kindness multiplier in operation.

DIRECTED

Rather than spreading your kindness to all and sundry, both the kindness and the multiplier increase in intensity when we focus the kindness. So this isn't about making faceless donations to charity.

This brings up another crucial point. The intention we hold when we perform the kindness should not be about what might bounce back for us. The intention of our kindness must be directed and channelled outwards.

SILENT

When we take on board the connection between kindness and intent, it's clear that nobody needs to be aware that we have been kind to them for the rebound effect to take place. So we can perform kindnesses without declaring to the world how wonderful we've been. We can even just go about our days in a kind manner, thinking kind thoughts and oozing kindness silently through our pores.

Unconsciously people will then sense an aura of kindness around you. You will look like a kind person and people will instantly place their trust in you. Uncannily, this kind of trust even leaks out from seemingly inanimate entities like web pages. People who visit your web site, or read a blog, just sense innately your level of kindness and compassion. This holds true even if the page they are looking at has nothing to do with kindness. If you are involved with marketing or sales, kindness should therefore be a central, and ideally silent, component of your strategy.

DISCRIMINATE

Kindness starts within. The ideal position for us to assume is just to be naturally kind and for it to become part of our intrinsic nature. This makes it become effortless. To help get to this blissful state, when starting out with our kindness strategy, it pays to be discriminate.

Some people might think it's a bit weird, or you that are somewhat crazy, if you are unconditionally kind to them.

When this happens it weakens your kindness field and can even take you backwards into a Danger Zone. Remember that just one kindness a day is all that's needed, so take baby steps at first.

REFLECTED

If we are naturally giving in nature, when kindness comes back our way, we may at first reject or refuse it. This is of course linked to any time spent in the Guilt Zone. Perhaps we feel we're not worthy or someone else should benefit from any reflected kindness.

This is a fundamental error and has the effect of breaking the chain and nullifying your initial kindness in the first place. So when someone is kind to you, give thanks and accept it gracefully. The kindness flow is then maintained and further amplified.

ZONING IN

So kindness is not a nice-to-have or something we do only on a Sunday. It is an integral part of being an evolved human being in this century and at this time. We then begin to live in a world filled altruism, benevolence, tolerance and understanding.

Patterns of behaviour we instigate in society today become embedded, integral and natural traits to be adopted by future generations. Being kind to someone today is a kindness that will ripple down the timelines. One day kindness might even be on the curriculum in schools.

[18]

The Loving Zone

BEING IN LOVE AND BEING OUT OF LOVE HAVE ONE COMMON ELEMENT - AND THAT'S US!

If we are not in love with who and what we are, it's a big call to expect someone else to love us.

This kind of self-love should not be confused with narcissism. It's the kind of love when we are really comfortable about being in our skin. We are confident, not arrogant and pleased with ourselves without being smug.

Love is different too from those other two four letter words beginning with "L" of 'Lust' and just a plain old 'Like'. Love that is 'lust-like' comes from our sacral and root mind centres and is largely derived from our body chemistry, as opposed to our higher minds.

While just liking someone, or something, is a great indicator in its own right. If we merely like something, we know for sure we aren't in love with it.

So when we are in the process of falling in love or being in love, it's worth checking where we are on our 'Lust-ometer' and 'Like-ometer'. If these are registering high, then it might be a sign our love is being clouded or diffused. Note though that many a relationship starts with a level of liking and can have a fair sprinkling of lust thrown in at the beginning.

It should be remembered of course that not all love has to have a conjugal element; some can be platonic. We can of course be equally in love with a thing or a situation as well as a person.

Being in and staying in the Loving Zone for any amount of time is both an art and a science. Those that pull this feat off will be happy in both personal and business relationships. It's the key to a long and happy life too.

Our heart centre does more than feel love, it is the place in our physiology where love is beamed out from. In the Eastern tradition, our heart centre is one of our main chakra points and the energy from these centres is now being detected by some open minded neuroscientists. Something remarkable happens though when we learn that we have an active 'mind centre' just behind our breast bone. We can take conscious control of it and perform what looks like magic.

Our heart centre contains a powerful and largely untapped ray that beams out in front of us and behind us like a vortex. When we fall in love with someone, unconsciously what happens is that our two heart rays intertwine into each other, rather like two spiral strands of DNA. Our language again gives it away as when this happens, "Two become one".

There is something even more powerful that we can do with this ray. We can use it to send love to ourselves or someone else's heart centre. If you are going into an antagonistic meeting, you can even soften the hearts of those attending in advance.

We can also use it to heal physical ailments and psychological issues both with ourselves and others. This also works across space and time. We can heal anyone anywhere on the planet in the past, the present and even the future. Note of course that, as for all magic, we must be ethical in its use. Permission must always be granted before remote healing is administered. If this all sounds a bit bizarre by the way, then listen to the Heart Ray Activation in the Getting in the Zone ecourse to experience the effect for yourself.

Exploration of the sub-zones of the Loving Zone allow us to see how we can be in love with ourselves, or someone or something, for the rest of our lives.

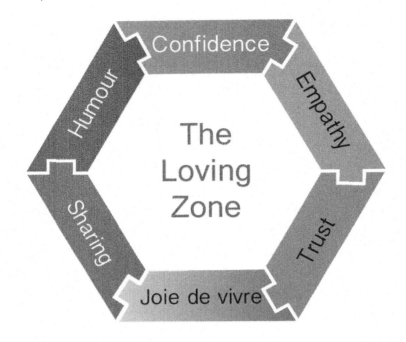

Confidence

When we ooze confidence without too much arrogance, we become very attractive. Combined with the right amount of self-love, less any narcissism, confidence makes people around us feel at ease.

When two suitably confident people meet, unconditional love can flow bidirectionally. If one person uses their confidence to dominate or subjugate the other, the seeds of discontent are sown.

HUMOUR

I am sure many Lonely Hearts ads to seek that perfect partner include the acronym - GSOH. Possessing a Good Sense of Humour, along with a healthy dose of self-depreciation, generates an ambience for love and mutual respect to flow.

While everyone likes a laugh, someone who fools around or jokes incessantly can be a bit of a pain. Quality as opposed to quantity is the key here. A GSOT - or Good Sense of Timing - is also very useful.

EMPATHY

For love to work, we have to empathise with those around us. Not only should we sense their mood and respond accordingly, we should also predict where a mood might be heading.

Fortunately we possess two ears and one mouth and this is a guide to the proportions in which we must use them. Many a person who has been listened to properly has been known to credit the listener as being a great conversationalist.

We should also listen to the subtle signals from our heart and gut minds. While they may not use language, they can tell us much and can always be trusted.

SHARING

One of the best things about being in love is having someone to share things with. This might be an experience, a bottle of wine or the last chocolate from the box.

It might also be an issue which is nicely encapsulated by the phrase, "a problem aired is a problem shared". Having someone to bounce off is a real luxury and something essential for good health. Not being able to get something off your chest can eventually lead to dis-ease.

TRUST

As you can see, real love has so many spin off benefits. Being able to rely on and trust someone is right up there with them.

Conversely betrayal of trust is probably the biggest undoer for so many bonds of love. This might not be infidelity. It might just be not doing what we promised to do when we promised to do it.

JOIE DE VIVRE

All love needs a certain amount of enthusiasm to give it momentum and direction. It can also carry an acceptable form of lust - a lust for life.

Often we have to take recourse to other languages to evoke just the right sentiment. For example, 'joy of life' sounds a little worthy and earnest when compared with 'joie de vivre'.

Likewise 'joie d'amour' is so much more evocative and sensuous than 'joy of love', which could have so many wrong connotations.

ZONING IN

When they sang "Love is a drug" and "Love is in the air", those songwriters were being more literal than we might first have thought. Love isn't a nice-to-have four letter word. It is a powerful force that can be used to heal too.

It's even possible that the mysterious missing Dark Energy and Dark Matter are actually some form of universal and all-pervasive love. Gravitational attraction is one of the weakest forces in nature but the one that stretches right across the Universe. Perhaps the Earth revolves around the Sun because it loves to. Perhaps our feet are held to the ground as we love to be bonded with Mother Earth.

I'd love for an enterprising and enquiring cosmologist to run with this notion to see where it might lead them.

[19]

The Happy Zone

OUR GENERAL LEVEL OF HAPPINESS IS A GREAT BAROMETER OF HOW WE ARE GETTING ALONG IN THE BEING ZONES.

When we complete customer satisfaction surveys, we often get asked how happy we are with the service. Whole nations are even ranked on their population's happiness quotient.

When we are asked how happy we are, we will be questioned on our relationships, our finances, our health, our work, our friends and our home. Few people perhaps will score 10 out of 10 in all these categories.

Remarkably, not many surveys seem to dare to ask the most pertinent question of all and that's to inquire as to how happy we are with ourselves.

When we are genuinely happy internally, we will find that all the externally measured happiness indices score highly as a matter of course.

It is putting the cart before the horse to base our happiness on external parameters. Many lottery winners would testify that money can't buy love and nor does it guarantee or generate happiness in itself.

Internal happiness though is not about being smug or being richer than our friends and neighbours. Neither is it about walking around in a meditative half-trance showering blessings around on all and sundry. It's also not limited to being happy in our own skin.

When we are truly happy, our mind, body and spirit are all on song. So as well as a healthy and pain-free body, our mind should be completely free of any of the thought forms found in the Danger Zones. Our spirit too will be shining as a result and evident in our creative output and even in our aura, be it imagined or perceived.

There are so many collateral benefits to being internally happy. We become less angry, less stressed and more productive. Those that are happy tend to live longer and enjoy more fulfilled lives. They look and act younger and people ask them what their secret is and even if they've had treatment.

While many religions espouse similar beliefs, in our increasingly secular society we are perhaps missing a set of Happiness Commandments.

Unlike the old style commandments with all their "shalt nots", they would of course be framed in the positive.

They should also be internally focused, without any associated fear or guilt about them being self-centred. When we are happy without being smug, those around us will be happy with and for us too.

As happiness is personal to each of us, I encourage each person to make up their own 'happiness commandments' and to stick them on a wall where they see them each day. They should be ranked in order of what makes us most happy first.

The sub-zones give some clues as to what such commandments should contain and to where they might lead us.

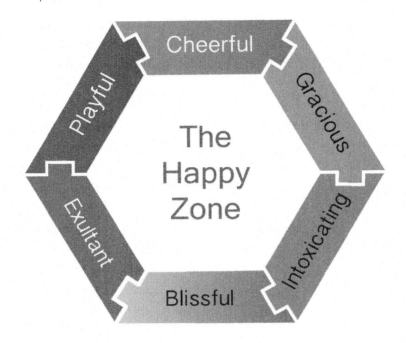

CHEERFUL

When we go about our days with a cheery disposition, we become 'radiators' not 'drains'. If you can see a person's aura, as we all can with little training, happy people positively glow and shine.

If an ache or pain surfaces to dim our happiness, the cheerful person merely sees it as a sign. They see any adversity as an exciting opportunity for learning. With this strategy, many things that would make others unhappy simply vapourise.

PLAYFUL

At school, learning is a serious business and any actual play is often limited to the playground. For example, maths couldn't possibly be fun, could it? I love showing children some magical properties of the number 9, so they can add two 6 digit numbers together in less than a second. As soon as you show them the trick, they can't wait to tell their friends.

When we later enter the workplace, whether as an employer, employee, supplier or customer, anything to do with commerce has to be deadly serious. If a bank manager smiled at you, you might wonder what was up!

It's time for humour to make not so much a comeback but to become an essential aspect of our day. Happy workers are so much more productive after all.

GRACIOUS

Happy people though shouldn't go around all day cracking jokes or playing tricks on people. That gets boring pretty quickly.

Happiness also spreads, without being overtly broadcast, from adopting a position and attitude of grace and lightness.

When things flow effortlessly without consternation or antagonism, it's a fabulous indicator that a contented person is at work. Build a whole work force of gracious people and your business will be unstoppable.

EXULTANT

The results of endeavours we achieve in a happy state of mind can take us to yet loftier heights. Our output reaches a class above what we produce while in a mediocre frame of mind.

In this state, what we do, what we produce and who we become may surprise even ourselves. We may wonder why we struggled so hard for so long when it was always so easy. When we love what we do, we never actually 'work' again after all.

INTOXICATING

As for all the zones, our state of mind and state of being affects our biochemistry. Like love, happiness quite literally is a drug that it is worth getting addicted to. A daily fix on this occasion is highly recommended.

It is actually this intoxication that makes happiness so infectious. We cannot help for this process to happen as our mirror neurons cause us to mimic the moods of those around us. This is how we learn.

What could be better than learning to be happy? If so, there is no school to go to per se. Just hang around more with happy people.

BLISSFUL

There are even higher states of happiness where immunity can be reached from the naysayers, and the Danger Zones in general.

When being in the Happy Zone becomes second nature, we take it as a given not an option. When you become happiness personified, there is no going back to the old ways. You become bliss-full.

Zoning In

Happiness is not a luxury. Neither should we be guilty about feeling happy. If we are happy while others aren't, it doesn't serve anyone if we descend into unhappiness with them. We should be sympathetic and empathetic for sure, but we should not let the misery of others make us unhappy. This serves nobody.

One of the main aims of this book is to help people be happier. By deconstructing some of our woes in each of the Danger Zones, it should become clear that the migration route to a happy life is to walk away from those zones and to inhabit some of the Doing and Being Zones.

If this simple and effective approach works for you, that would make me very happy indeed.

[20]

The Chillout Zone

THESE DAYS WE ARE SPOILED FOR CHOICE WITH
A MYRIAD OF WAYS TO RELAX.

For decades now, we've been able to watch TV, take in a movie
or listen to music. Since the end of the last century, all sorts of
entertainment has been on tap via the Internet. More recently,
more and more people use their smartphones and tablet
computers as portable entertainment centres. These are all
great ways to let our hair down and, for many of us, are just a
mere finger tap away.

While a certain amount of relaxation and enjoyment can be
gained from such activities, quite often we are not chilling out
that much.

If we watch a thriller, play a combat game or listen to heavy
rock, a rampant chemical cocktail will be mixed in our body. If
we tune into a football game, or listen to a classical symphony,
we will fire off the same emotional centres all over our body as
if we were actually on the pitch, or perhaps conducting the
orchestra.

With this kind of entertainment, we may well relax and enjoy ourselves. What we're actually doing is 'chilling in' to an alternative reality, created by others, in an attempt to tune out of our own life. Sometimes these activities can drag us into the Addiction Zone.

Of course another way to relax is to have an afternoon nap. When we sleep, we also check out of reality and recharge our batteries.

When we want to operate at our peak in either a Doing or Being Zone, there is a form of relaxation, commonly referred to as meditation, that takes us to another level and a new place. For the most part, it's free, accessible to all and a great antidote to any of the Danger Zones.

Before I started meditating in my mid-40's, like many people, I was quite cynical about the whole idea. The inner demons surfaced and I worried I wouldn't be able to make my mind go quiet. Perhaps I was just being silly and was wasting valuable time I could well use elsewhere. Did I really have time to waste doing nothing?

Nowadays I positively luxuriate and look forward to some 'me time' with a mind quiet of chatter each day. Indeed, if I don't get it, I seem to have a worse day. I mentioned earlier that it could be seen as a form of addiction, and therefore a zone we don't want to get stuck in. I prefer to see it as a discipline, a practice and a way of life.

So if there is one addiction you allow into your life, this should be it. It's safe and it promotes good health, vitality and even increases our longevity. It's thought that every minute you meditate, you add a minute to your life. If this is true, it's madness not to meditate as we will get any investment of time back.

Getting our thoughts to stop though at first seems an impossible task. Even when we are asleep, the raging lion of our unconscious mind bubbles uncontrollably to the surface in the form of dreams.

From the minute we awaken until we drop back into the Land of Nod, our inner dialogue fires up. There is so much noise in our busy world, it's hard to switch off. Even when we could be silent, we have the radio on in the background or switch the TV on when we get in from work. We fill our world with noise.

So what is this mysterious meditative state all about and how do we get into this special version of the Chillout Zone?

Well the good news is that everyone of us is a natural meditator. If you have ever driven home on a familiar route, and not remembered how you got home, then you had entered a form of meditative state. If you were in a boring meeting and your mind went elsewhere, you were getting into the Chillout Zone naturally.

The meditative state can be accessed with either eyes open or eyes closed. The Chillout Zone too is not necessarily a place of quiet and rest.

For a sports person to perform at their peak, they must reach this level of relaxation with crowds roaring around them. Many an artist or writer will produce their best work while in the Chillout Zone listening to their favourite music.

There are two tricks we can use to make our mind go quiet. They are both based on the principle that the normal human mind can only hold one thought at a time.

The first technique is to focus on something like the breath, a candle flame or a spot on the wall, such that our internal dialogue gets replaced by the attention we are paying to 'the thing'. That 'thing' too can be a mantra, which is a short phrase that we repeat over and over in our head or out loud. Counting sheep on sleepless nights uses this principle.

We can reach an even deeper level of meditation by thinking about any thought that happens to come in, at the time it comes in. As a result of doing this, our conscious mind gives up trying 'to think' and goes quiet on us. The ecourse that accompanies this book that will guide you through practicing these techniques. See the Getting in the Zone section for more details.

There are other disciplines that you can take up, like yoga and Tai Chi, to enhance your experience in the Chillout Zone.

The sub-zones of the Chillout Zones are somewhat different and more ethereal than others. They are more like qualities than places or regions.

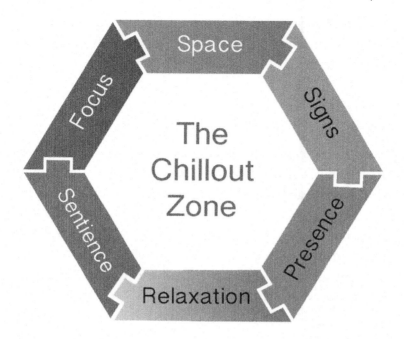

SPACE

What happens when we enter this zone under our own volition is that we create space around us.

An Olympic athlete might be watched by millions but, as far as they are concerned, they are alone in their own bubble.

When writing, I have noticed how the phone never seems to ring until I finish a chapter, such is the power of the intention field we emit when we are in this zone.

While learning to get and stay in this zone therefore, it's important to create space around you so you can perform.

This means to create physical space for you to 'strut your stuff' and enough quality time for you to hone your craft and produce your output.

Focus

Once we create space, we have to apply focus and this focus is simultaneously of two types. We have to focus on the minute detail of our craft. Every word for a writer, every brush stroke for an artist and the nuances of the breeze for an athlete. At the same time, we have to hold the global vision. The writer has a sense of that word in the context of the whole book. The artist has the whole canvas in mind. That athlete is aware of all other competitors around them.

Fortunately most of us are equipped with the perfect organ to pull this feat off. It is our brain, and specifically as mentioned before, the left brain which concerns itself with detail and the right brain that holds the whole vision.

Signs

One of the most magical features of being in the Chillout Zone is that our serendipity goes up several notches. We become incredibly lucky and fortuitous.

When we are simultaneously zoned in and zoned out, we notice that we are surrounded by signs which provide sources of information and inspiration.

When our internal chatter is high, it has the effect of blocking out the 'blooming obvious'. When I work with writers who are looking for the perfect book title, they often mention their eventual title unconsciously in something they say. When we speak, we are often not listening to the actual content of what we are saying.

SENTIENCE

Chilling out in this manner does not mean copping out and walking away from responsibility. It means taking full ownership of each and every thought and feeling in our mind and body.

We are all sentient star dust and the remnants of supernovas that exploded billions of years ago. The atoms of our body haven't assembled at random. They have come together for a purpose and that's our creative and entrepreneurial output and our ability to perform to our best at whatever it is that we do. When we are aware of this fact and take ownership of it, we transcend to a new place.

PRESENCE

In this new place, people take notice of us. Perhaps unconsciously, they pick up on the fact that billions of atoms have assembled into this sentient being that is us. What's more, they sense that this being is on a mission and has a sense of purpose.

Without making a big song and dance over what we are about, we broadcast with gravitas. We walk in grace and with purpose.

RELAXATION

Now this might all sound a bit worthy so it's also important not to take ourselves too seriously while doing all of this. We are currently one of around seven billion beings who are potentially capable of mimicking our achievements.

We have to be relaxed in our own skin and relaxed about being a small but significant part of the collective. The classic form of ego has no place in the Chillout Zone.

Zoning In

In time, if we follow a meditative practice, we end up being in the Chillout Zone more than we are out of it. If we are in conversation, or out for a walk, we end up being chilled out and relaxed.

We soon learn that chilling out is not something we do at the start or end of a day. It's something we become!

The Magic Zone

MAGIC IS MAKING A BIT OF A COMEBACK IN THE WORLD. WE CAN SEE IT IN OUR CULTURE ON FILMS AND TV AND, IF YOU REALLY TUNE IN, YOU CAN ALSO FEEL IT IN THE WATER AND SMELL IT IN THE AIR.

There are different degrees of magic. If a Victorian came forward into our time today and saw someone talking to, or even seeing, someone on their mobile phone on the other side of the world, they would think that was magic. The same may be true for us if we could hop forward a century or so to see what magic our grandchildren will come up with.

Arthur C. Clarke was quoted to have said, "Any sufficiently advanced technology is indistinguishable from magic."

In some ways, modern technology is similar to traditional alchemical magic. Indeed the roots of all chemistry, and a fair bit of physics, began with alchemists concocting all manner of strange brews in their cauldrons. Even Isaac Newton was reputed to have been an alchemist.

Today's metaphysics is tomorrow's physics. Semiconductors work using quantum magic. Oil, gas or coal is used to create electricity - or electrickery. A television or computer display works by taking that electrical energy and transmuting it into light. That is alchemy in a nutshell.

Most peoples' experience of magic comes from seeing sleight-of-hand magicians. Skilled magicians of this kind are fabulously entertaining and bring out the inner child in all of us. For the most part, we know it's a trick but we suspend our belief and let our mind think it's real.

There are also a breed of sleight-of-mind magicians who appear to read minds and tell you things they could not possibly know about you. Again, these wizards are both engaging and beguiling. Most of them simply bamboozle us by diverting our attention away from the obvious mechanism they use to perform their tricks.

The Magic Zone though refers to a more subtle, practical and accessible kind of magic. The first form of it allows us to lead what looks like a charmed and abundant life.

Masters of the Magic Zone rarely visit the Danger Zones. They spend a lot of time in the Doing Zones. They are creative entrepreneurs, and sometimes performers, who are adept at making things happen in the real world. Most crucially though, they have mastered the Being Zones.

They are loving, kind, happy and chilled out. Many are natural healers.

Opportunity abounds for them and creativity oozes from their pores. They are good people to have in your company - be that in a personal relationship or a business context.

It is no accident that this is the last zone in this edition of this particular book as all other zones lead to it. It is not so much a separate zone but the summation of all the Doing and Being Zones, whilst also being an annulling force to any of the Danger Zones.

When you spend time in the Magic Zone, life becomes a breeze and you become surrounded by abundance. You always have enough money to do anything you want. Clients find you and time expands around you so you can get what you want done, when you want to do it.

What is even more magical though is that, after spending a little time in this state, you start to realise that even greater levels of magic are at your finger tips. To explain how this works, just imagine a two dimensional world without an 'up'. This 'Flatland' is occupied by two dimensional geometric shapes like squares, circles and triangles.

As a three dimensional being, you can easily peer into this world. If you were a bit devilish, you could reach in from above and, as they have no 'up', they wouldn't see you coming. You could pluck an unsuspecting circle out of a crowd of Flatlanders and they would think that circle had disappeared. What's more, the circle would now be in this wondrous three dimensional world and be having its mind slightly blown at what it could see.

When the circle returns to Flatland, it could regale its fellows with tales of a strange land. They might think the circle has gone round the figurative bend and become somewhat misshapen and oval.

The true magician in Cubeland (i.e. our world) is a bit like our circle in Flatland. They have experienced things that only make sense if our four dimensional space and time is the tip of a multi-dimensional iceberg. Not only has a true magician seen these worlds but they can also communicate with them and use their forces to effect a different kind of magic in our world.

All magic stops being magical once you know how the trick is done. This kind of magic is extremely effective and powerful and, for this reason, the secrets of how to invoke it are only known by a few.

All magic can be used for good and not so good purposes. There is a bit of a magical safeguard though. If you find yourself in the Magic Zone but dispense your magic for your own selfish purposes, it will bounce back on you. That said, adoption of the qualities of the sub-zones is great preparation for those who want to take the next steps.

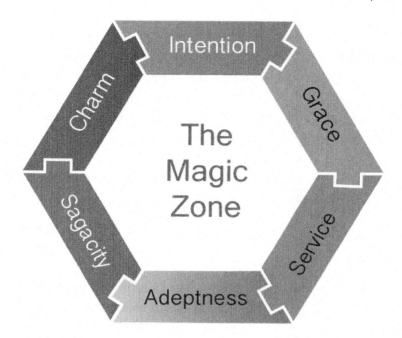

INTENTION

To ensure your magic doesn't bounce back on you, it is vital that you hold the highest intention for your aims. The way to get to high intention is to think of the best outcome for any spell you might invoke and then to think of what would be even better when it works. Then think what could be even better still and so forth.

Never do anything that betters your position at the expense of others and aim for everything you do to be ecological and ethical.

CHARM

There are 'real' magicians, sorcerers and wizards all over the planet, especially so at this time of transition and transformation. Unlike stage magicians, they don't advertise who they are and what they can actually do. Indeed some of them don't even know what they are.

Those who are cogniscent of their powers go about their work with charm and can be quite beguiling to be around.

GRACE

As well as charm, modern day alchemists breeze through life with ease and grace. They are masters at controlling their auric field so could be in a room with you and you wouldn't particularly notice them.

The evidence they leave behind is the only tell tale sign you have met with one of them. If you find someone helps you make something happen for you that is beyond your wildest dreams, you know you've met a 'real' magician.

If you do spot their beneficial influence on your life, it pays dividends to thank them, even if the thanks is spoken internally and silently in your mind.

Sagacity

Real magicians are wise beyond their years. If you come across a particularly bright pupil at school ,who is years ahead of their peers, you are quite possibly in the presence of an old soul going around the loop again.

When you wield immense power, it pays to be wise and mindful of its potential impact on others when unleashed. This is why the best magic is done with the minimum of fuzz and pizzazz. The best tricks are the ones where you quite know what just happened.

Adeptness

As for stage magicians who make things look easy, a real magician masters their craft through continual practice and development.

To migrate from being a simulator of magic to being a proponent of real magic is just one rung on the ladder of advancement. There is a near infinity of rungs yet to climb and an infinity of tricks to be learned.

Service

With great power comes great responsibility and humility. The real magician knows they are not actually powerful at all.

They have just learned the tricks of how to tap into the power available to us all from both the higher and lower dimensions. They know the real trick they have pulled off is how to act as a connector and conduit from the Above to the Below.

They are in service on the Earth Plane for the good of humanity, and indeed all life forms on the planet and for Mother Earth herself. It is not so much that a magician ever achieves a particular level of adeptness, but that certain skills and abilities have been conferred on them because they can be trusted with that level of power.

The magic doesn't so much come from them as through them.

Zoning In

It is in the interests of safety for the readers of this book that no real magical secrets have been dispensed on this trip around the zones.

Exploration of the zones though is great preparation to those who want to live a charmed and magical existence, and as a precursor to stepping well and truly up to the plate.

The Magic Zone is the most powerfully infectious zone. When you enter it, all sorts of wonderment will enter your world and you will astound and amaze the people around you.

To discover more about this realm, all we have to do is to be open to the possibility of its existence. When we are ready, the keys will appear, just like magic.

Super Z◯nes

THE OBSERVANT AND ENQUIRING READER MAY HAVE WONDERED IF THERE IS ANY SIGNIFICANCE TO EACH ZONE BEING COMPRISED OF SIX SUB-ZONES.

As any bee or apiarist knows, the six-sided hexagon allows maximum packing density for a honeycomb of chambers in the hive for new larvae to grow. At the same time, the hexagon is virtually incompressible and therefore incredibly strong and resilient.

So this shape was intentionally chosen when I started this book to allow further experimentation with the zones. I was purely 'driven to think' of this idea one day somewhat ironically when I was driving in that chilled out state along a familiar route. I did not at that time fully explore the possibilities opened up by adopting this meta-strategy.

Only when writing this chapter did the full comprehension of the significance of this seed notion become clear.

The idea that came in was that the 18 zones described in this book could be combined and fused to form complex honeycombs of zones, which also encapsulate all attributes of their sub-zones. I've called them Super Zones.

For the mathematically inclined, there are 18 factorial composite zones that can be formed. This means there are billions of theoretical Super Zones that can be synthesised - 6,402,373,705,728,000 in fact. So if you tried out one permutation of just these 18 zones per second, you would have to live for over 2 million years to go through them all. There are even more subtle variations to be fabricated still when you start to flip and rotate the orientation of each zone.

Some fun can be had however with relatively simple Super Zones formed of just a few other zones. Just combining three zones together allows us to synthesise new ways of approaching a task or endeavour.

Zones of seven are powerful agents for change and transformation. The zone in the centre can become the Master Zone supported by those around it. This type of Super Zone brings amazing enlightenment to its designer.

Conversely, if the central zone of seven is one of the Danger Zones, its negativity can be annulled by choosing the right zones to envelope it. This allows us to create powerful mechanisms for change in our lives.

This chapter contains just a few examples. I invite you to play and to let me know what you come up with.

A SIMPLE SUPER ZONE

Let's imagine you were launching an online dating agency and wanted some inspiration in the design phase. You will need to be creative to make your site different from the rest. You will need to be entrepreneurial in business. As the site is all about joining hearts together, you will also need to sprinkle a bit of love into the mix. So here's the first example of a Super Zone to help steer this business forward.

This new composite zone shows you the values the business can use to build its brand. It gives you the qualities your team will need to be successful. It also indicates what qualities you can bring to your clients so that they may find love. You can create copy for brochures and web sites based on the key words of the sub-zones.

For example, by helping your clients improve their luck, you give them optimism. Some added spark will give them more exposure. This will increase their confidence and help them be less desperate and more empathic. Using a more whole-istic approach in dating will eventually lead to longer lasting relationships.

So, by using this kind of language, your site will stand out from the pack and your clients will become more attractive as a result. You will make the more complete.

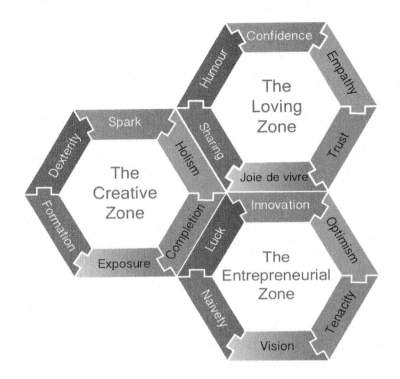

MEGA DANGER ZONES

As mentioned, we often occupy more than one zone at a time. This is especially true when we enter the Danger Zones. So someone who is in the Addiction Zone might also have one foot in the Guilt Zone. They may also be inhabiting the Anger Zone. They may be both angry at themselves and the world in general.

When we live in multiple Danger Zones, rational logic can get thrown out of the window as we create a distorted view of the world for ourselves.

This type of Mega Danger Zone gives a better picture of what might be going on in the world of an addict. They may be exhibiting psychotic tendencies from the Anger Zone. They may feel guilt because they have disgraced themselves.

As a result, what might happen is that we treat the psychosis not the underlying reason for the addiction in the first place.

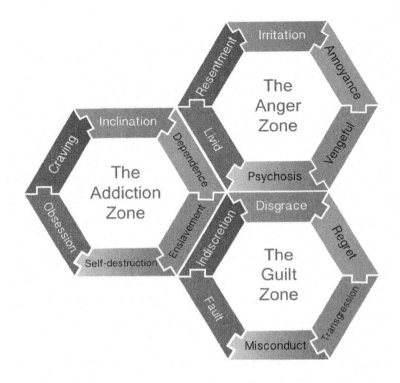

HOW TO NEUTRALISE DANGER ZONES

This leads us to a new way of exiting the Danger Zones permanently. When faced with dealing with a number of Danger Zones at the same time, it's challenging to take them all on at once. Perhaps the addiction arose as a result of being angry at the system or it stemmed from a hidden guilt from childhood abuse.

So what we do is to take a single Danger Zone and surround it with any six of the Doing and Being Zones, as shown. I have taken three of the Doing Zones and alternated them with three of the Being Zones. I did not give much thought to this and my intuition is that any Danger Zone can be neutralised with any six Doing or Being Zones.

Remember too that the 18 zones in this book represent a small selection of many possible zones.

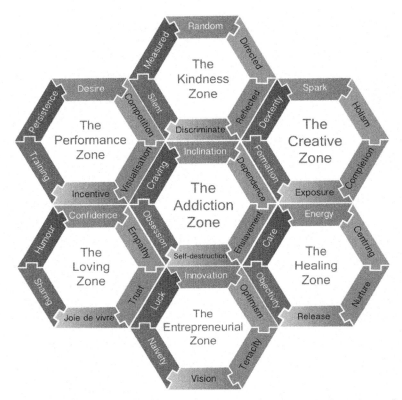

So what we have now done is matched the six sub-zones of Addiction with attributes from the surrounding zones. This allows us to redefine the behaviour of someone who is addicted as shown in this new Super Zone.

So starting at the top of the Addiction Zone and going clockwise, we can morph the old addiction into a way of being which is much more productive and healthy.

Where we previously had an Inclination towards our addiction, we can choose to Discriminate and Drive our focus away from it by being Kind to ourselves and others.

Where we had a Dependence, we can Formulate a way to Control it by being Creative.

Where we were Enslaved, we can take Care of ourselves by gaining Mastery of our thought forms. This is the most powerful self-delivery Healing mechanism around.

Where we were Self-Destructive, we Redirect our energies in an Entrepreneurial activity.

Our Obsessions are replaced with small Successes as we find Love both in ourselves and those around us.

Our Cravings transmute into being merely Requisites as we become addicted to fulfilling needs that allow us to Perform at our best again.

In this way the old sub-zones of addiction get replaced by six new attributes which lead us towards a new coping strategy. In time, this new way of being becomes the New Addiction.

You can try this exercise out yourself with any of the other Danger Zones.

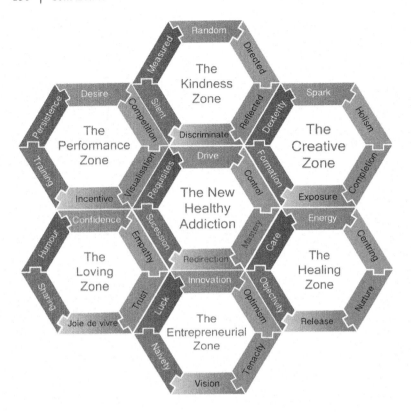

THE POWER OF MASTER ZONES

As mentioned, we can also assemble Super Zones with a central Master Zone, surrounded and strengthened by supporting zones. So let's say we were involved in live performance of some form, we could then choose what qualities we would like to support us in constructing our persona and in entertaining or educating our audience.

Before each live performance, we could glance or ideally meditate on this Super Zone to get ourselves into the perfect mind space for optimum delivery. This is the one I use to prepare for an interview or when I deliver a workshop.

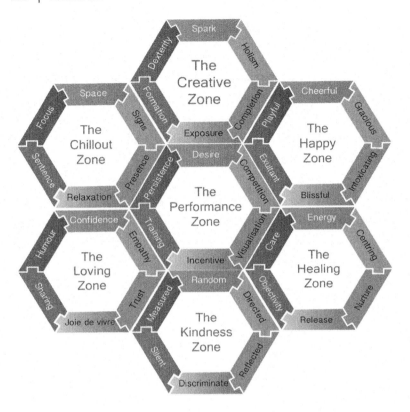

While this might all seem merely as linguistic fun, and perhaps construed as a cunning sleight-of-mind trick, there is something important to remember. The thoughts and words that go around in our head are the prime modifiers of our behaviour. They make the difference between having a bad or a good day.

When we change our thoughts, we change our mind. When we change our mind, we change the world.

WHEN WE ARE IN THE ZONE, THE WORLD DOESN'T JUST HAPPEN TO US, IT HAPPENS BECAUSE OF US.

THIS BOOK IS COMPLIMENTED BY MULTIMEDIA RESOURCES TO HELP YOU GET AND STAY IN THE ZONE.

GETTING IN THE ZONE ECOURSE

The main resource centre is a companion ecourse to this book which includes several mind-altering audio visualisations, as mentioned in the book, to help you get in the zone.

You'll find loads of interviews with experts in the various zones. It also contains lectures on increasing creativity and productivity using Whole Brain Thinking and Whole Mind Thinking techniques.

The course is moderately priced but is absolutely free for readers of book using the redemption code THEZONE

www.udemy.com/get-in-the-zone

GETTING INTO THE DECISION ZONE

Making the right decision at exactly the right time can save us much heartache and bags of time.

One of the reasons it is so difficult at times is that our thoughts don't all emanate from our heads. The Flavours of Thought ecourse explores the true nature, quality and sources of our thoughts - you will never think about them quite the same way again.

Use the redemption code THEZONE to get 33% off the normal price.

www.udemy.com/flavours-of-thought

Getting into The Time Zone and Chillout Zone

The Bending Time ecourse shows you how to get more done in less time. It's a magical tour around the Time Zone. Find out how your consciousness, your breath and the passage of time are all interlinked. Discover how to tune into 'future memories' and how to send messages to yourself across time.

With over 3 hours of relaxing and hypnotic audio meditations, you will find out how to get in and to stay in the Chillout Zone too.

Use the same redemption code THEZONE to get 33% off the normal price

www.udemy.com/bending-time

About the author

TOM GAINED AN HONOURS DEGREE IN ELECTRICKERY, BEFORE EMBARKING A CAREER AS A BBC BROADCAST ENGINEER, WORKING WITH THE MAGIC OF TELEVISION.

In his mid-forties, he wrote a book by accident. As a result, he ended up becoming an author's mentor and a specialist at removing writer's block. Nowadays he also clears block of a more general kind, which may have lead to illness and dis-ease.

He lives with his life partner in the Surrey Hills in the UK, which is just the perfect place to go out for a dog walk in order to get in the Zone.

FIND OUT MORE ABOUT TOM ON HIS WEB SITE
WWW.TOMEVANS.CO

Acknowledgements

THANKS TO ALL THE PEOPLE WHO HELPED BRINGING THIS BOOK INTO THE WORLD AND FOR BEING PART OF MY JOURNEY EXPLORING EACH OF THESE ZONES.

To Louise for her innate wisdom and unerring faith and support.

To Jackie Walker and Denise Harris-Heigho for being the best sounding boards an author could wish for. To Jayney Goddard for picking up the baton so quickly.

To Paul Chaplin for his perspicacity.

To all explorers who push the boundaries and chart new territories.

Also by Tom Evans

NON-FICTION WORKS AVAILABLE IN PRINT AND FOR
EREADERS

An exploration of what we know,
what we don't know and what sort
of world we could know ...

*"... short, elegant and perfectly formed.
A small book with a big impact ..."*

This We Know

Ever wondered where ideas came
from and how to stop the best ones
from getting away?

*"... a fabulously evocative book full of humour,
wisdom and insight. Simply inspiring ..."*

The Art & Science of Light Bulb Moments

A contemporary exploration and exposition of the wisdom contained in the Major Arcana of the Tarot ...

"... this has become my go-to book any time I need guidance and support"

Flavours of Thought

Hidden in the Minor Arcana of the Tarot is the secret of who we really are and where we might be going ...

"... another mind-bending and inspiring read. Get ready for a wild ride."

Planes of Being

An immersive guide to clearing writer's block and unleashing your Creative Muse ...

"... packed with practical techniques to ensure your blocks are a thing of the past"

Blocks

SHORT STORIES FOR EREADERS

A poetic trilogy about one family
told in just 99 stanzas ...

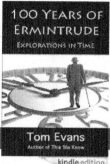

"Stunning. I cried. That's all."

100 Years of Ermintrude

A future history of planet Earth,
how we got here and where we
might be heading ...

*"A good page turner and syfy at it's best,
a book I'll re-read again and again."*

Soulwave

tomevans
author | bookwright | catalyst

WWW.TOMEVANS.CO

CPSIA information can be obtained at www.ICGtesting.com
Printed in the USA
BVOW06s1947131016

464954BV00008B/79/P